BELIEVE TO SUCCEED LIKE AZIM PREMJI

Rajiv Agarwal is a family business consultant with more than twenty years of experience. Considered a leading expert on family business in India, he has advised more than 1,500 families on succession, strategy and continuity. Currently a professor of Family Business, Strategy and Entrepreneurship at S.P. Jain Institute of Management & Research (SPJIMR), Mumbai, which is also his alma mater, Agarwal pursued his PhD from BITS Pilani and is an alumnus of Harvard Business School. He has been the visiting professor at IIM Kozhikode and IIM Indore, and expert advisor on the Board of Academics, Department of Management, Nirma University, Ahmedabad. He also writes for various publications on topics related to family business.

Also by the same author

Think, Lead & Strategize like Kumar Mangalam Birla
Lead with Purpose like Anand Mahindra
Succeed to Inspire like the Tatas

BELIEVE TO SUCCEED LIKE AZIM PREMJI

RAJIV AGARWAL

Published by
Rupa Publications India Pvt. Ltd 2019
7/16, Ansari Road, Daryaganj
New Delhi 110002

Sales centres:
Allahabad Bengaluru Chennai
Hyderabad Jaipur Kathmandu
Kolkata Mumbai

Copyright © Rajiv Agarwal 2019

The views and opinions expressed in this book are the author's
own and the facts are as reported by him which have been
verified to the extent possible, and the publishers are not in
any way liable for the same.

All rights reserved.

No part of this publication may be reproduced, transmitted,
or stored in a retrieval system, in any form or by any means,
electronic, mechanical, photocopying, recording or otherwise,
without the prior permission of the publisher.

ISBN: 978-93-5333-766-7

First impression 2019

10 9 8 7 6 5 4 3 2 1

The moral right of the author has been asserted.

Printed at Replika Press Pvt. Ltd, India

This book is sold subject to the condition that it shall not,
by way of trade or otherwise, be lent, resold, hired out, or otherwise
circulated, without the publisher's prior consent, in any form of
binding or cover other than that in which it is published.

CONTENTS

Preface vii

Introduction xi

History xiii

1. Azim Premji: The Person Be Detail-oriented, and Humble   1
2. Frugality   10
3. Integrity and Corporate Governance   19
4. Dedication to Values   31
5. Willingness to Experiment and Learn   35
6. What Gets Measured Gets Done   40
7. Lead by Example: Be a Role Model to Emulate the Behaviour That You Want Others to Follow   46
8. Diversify and Seize Opportunities   51

9. Train and Mentor Your People Well	63
10. Make an Impact with the Wealth That You Give Away	79
11. Summary of Learnings	97
Annexure 1	102
Annexure 2	104
Annexure 3	106
Annexure 4	109
Acknowledgements	114

PREFACE

I began writing this book, with trepidation, in the middle of the year 2019. Given Azim Premji's reputation for media shyness, I was not sure whether I would get the information I required. But I ventured forth anyway, since I believed that his story was not adequately covered and it was one which needed to be told.

I was fortunate, as just then he had announced he was stepping down from Wipro and the media was filled with information covering this momentous event. But my research showed that there was still very little background information on him in the public domain. Keeping these limitations in mind, I still attempted to write this book.

Readers would be advised to note that this work is based purely and solely on information available in the public domain. Hence, it may suffer from the limitations of being restricted to what is being reported therein. Due to this, there could be errors or misstatements, and readers are advised to treat this work accordingly.

The sole purpose of this book is to serve as an educational tool for aspiring managers to learn from the leadership decisions of Azim Premji. I have given my interpretation of the actions at the end of every chapter. While it is again based on reported facts, readers should also be advised that it is easy to comment on instances post-facto, and there could be other factors that we may not be aware of since we are relying on third-party quoted information. In any case, I hope that this serves as an inspiration to future managers.

THE PREMJI FAMILY TREE

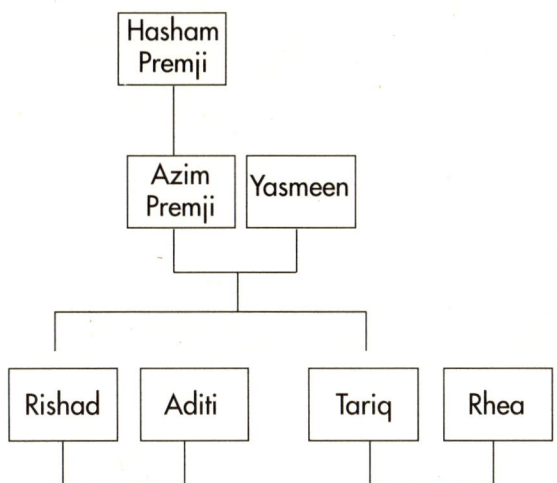

INTRODUCTION

The story of Azim Premji and his journey encompasses a fifty-three-year-long career with Wipro, as it transitioned from a small vegetable oil firm to a $8.5 billion information technology giant.[1] It is a story worth narrating.

Premji is, perhaps, one of the best examples of a media-shy billionaire who is successful, yet not a very prominent personality in the media—entirely by his choice.

The roots of serving society run deep in the Premji family.

If his success and achievements can be an inspiration to the many young managers who are seeking to better their lives and careers, his generosity redefines the concept of capitalism. Capitalism has always been regarded as the exploitation of resources and (sometimes) people for the sole purpose of enriching the individual and/or family. Now, it has one more purpose, which is to ensure that the creation of wealth has a

---

[1] 'Opinion: The Blazer of Diverse Trials to a Greater Goal', *Livemint*, 9 June 2019, https://www.livemint.com/opinion/online-views/opinion-the-blazer-of-diverse-trails-to-a-greater-goal-1560104111223.html

nobler objective—to impact society in a meaningful manner. The gargantuan size of his giveaway, coupled with his intention to ensure that it is being used in an impactful manner, shows his patriotic and altruistic intent, which is exemplary and admirable.

That is just one of the stories—perhaps the biggest—which surrounds the enigma that is Azim Premji. And that is all the more reason why his story needs to be told.

HISTORY

ॐ

Azim Premji is perhaps one of India's biggest entrepreneurs, and also a significant force in philanthropy.

WIPRO Limited was started as the Western India Vegetable Products Limited under the leadership of Mohamed Hasham Premji[1] in 1945. It was making vegetable and refined oils in Amalner, a small town in what is now northern Maharashtra. It filed for an initial public offering (IPO) in February 1946[2] and was listed on the Bombay Stock Exchange (BSE).

---

[1] The spelling 'Hasham' is taken from the Wipro Annual Report, 2003–2004, pg. 48, based on the spelling in Mr Premji's signature. There are other sources on the Internet who spell the name differently. Also, this is used in Bloomberg (https://www.bloomberg.com/billionaires/profiles/azim-h-premji/).

[2] Harish Puppala and Rakesh Sharma, 'Digging Deeper—Azim Premji: The End of an Era', Moneycontrol.com, accessed 13 June 2019, https://www.moneycontrol.com/news/podcast/digging-deeper-azim-premji-the-end-of-an-era-4090341.html; Varun Sood and Sundeep Khanna, 'Making of Azim Premji: The Philanthropist', *Livemint*, 24 June 2019, accessed 28 June 2019, https://www.livemint.com/companies/people/making-of-azim-premji-the-philanthropist-1561390035003.html

Premji's grandfather was an entrepreneur who had built up one of India's largest bulk rice trading companies in India. He was known as the Rice King of Burma.[3] His son, Hasham, (Azim Premji's father), worked for him for some time, before starting a venture of his own, a manufacturing and distribution company called Western India Vegetable Products in 1945.[4]

A story, which may be apocryphal, is that after the Partition of India, Mohammad Ali Jinnah had invited Hasham Premji to move to Pakistan, and had offered him a cabinet minister's position. But Premji had turned down the request, choosing to stay back in India since they had roots in Bombay (now Mumbai).[5]

However, Hasham Premji focused less on running the business and more on the nuances of policymaking. He devoted most of his energies in lobbying the national government to deregulate the food grains industry, besides serving on a few

---

[3] Anvar Alikhan, 'The Wrong 'Un Keeps Its Line', *Outlook*, 5 November 2012, accessed 23 September, 2019, https://www.outlookindia.com/magazine/story/the-wrong-un-keeps-its-line/282730. Askhay Sawai, 'From Food to Philanthropy: Retirement Tales of Azim Premji and Yuvraj Singh', *The Economic Times*, 18 January 2019, accessed 30 June 2019 https://economictimes.indiatimes.com/magazines/panache/from-food-to-philanthropy-retirement-tales-of-azim-premji-and-yuvraj-singh/articleshow/69835080.cms

[4] Steve Hamm, *Bangalore Tiger, How Indian Tech Upstart Wipro Is Rewriting the Rules of Global Competition*, Tata McGraw-Hill, India, 2007, pg. 32

[5] Yaroslav Trofimov, 'How a Muslim Billionaire Thrives in Hindu India', *The Wall Street Journal*, 11 September 2007, accessed 29 June 2019, https://www.wsj.com/articles/SB118947228823323260; Moneycontrol.com, accessed 30 June 2019, https://www.moneycontrol.com/news/podcast/digging-deeper-azim-premji-the-end-of-an-era-4090341.html

industry Boards. He became the chairman of the Bombay Electricity Board. He was also a Board member of the Reserve Bank of India, the State Bank of India and the Life Insurance Corporation of India.[6]

In August 1966, at the age of twenty-one, Azim Premji was forced to make a career-defining move while studying engineering in his second year at Stanford University, in the United States (US). He was informed that his father had passed away after a heart attack. He was fifty-one at the time. Left with no alternative, Azim had to put aside his dream of being a policymaker at the World Bank and helping to develop the Third World. Instead, he returned to India and took over the family business, deep-diving into the minutiae of saving a troubled company in a protected economy.[7] Little did he realize at the time that he would play a role that would impact the lives of thousands of children in the future, in a way that no one could imagine!

The young Azim felt duty-bound to respect his father's wishes and began to run the business. At the time, the company was publicly listed, which was rare in those times, and had about 350 employees with just $3 million in revenues.[8]

Azim took his responsibilities very seriously and began

---

[6] Podcast, 'Digging Deep—Giving and Growing: The Story of Wipro & Azim Premji', Moneycontrol.com, accessed 30 June 2019, https://www.moneycontrol.com/news/business/companies/podcast-digging-deep-giving-and-growing-the-story-of-wipro-azim-premji-2660341.html

[7] Steve Hamm, *Bangalore Tiger, How Indian Tech Upstart Wipro is Rewriting the Rules of Global Competition,* pg. 32, Tata McGraw-Hill, India, 2007

[8] Ibid.

learning on the job. He had to study concepts of business, a subject that he had never taken during his studies at Stanford. He learnt from textbooks recommended by a professor at a reputed management school in Mumbai. He built his business using modern practices and principles that he read about. He also got advice from his existing staff, not exactly the dynamic managers one would desire, but they knew the business well.[9] He brought in management graduates whose expertise was used in various decisions, from simplifying the packaging of Vanaspati to distributing and marketing it, amongst the newer sections of rural consumers.[10]

He introduced proper processes and more accurate systems which resulted in his company turning around. He took charge of the family business and soon diversified into bakery fats, soaps, toiletries, lighting products, and even started a hydraulic cylinders business.

Earlier, at Stanford, Premji had to work hard to catch up, since he lagged behind his classmates. He learnt to compete, and soon worked hard and set his eyes on always being in the top 20 per cent of his class.[11] At Wipro, he used the same

---

[9] Steve Hamm, *Bangalore Tiger, How Indian Tech Upstart Wipro is Rewriting the Rules of Global Competition*, pg. 32, Tata McGraw-Hill, India, 2007

[10] Podcast, 'Digging Deep—Giving and Growing: The Story of Wipro & Azim Premji', Moneycontrol.com, accessed 30 June 2019, https://www.moneycontrol.com/news/business/companies/podcast-digging-deep-giving-and-growing-the-story-of-wipro-azim-premji-2660341.html

[11] Steve Hamm, *Bangalore Tiger, How Indian Tech Upstart Wipro Is Rewriting the Rules of Global Competition*, pg. 32, Tata McGraw-Hill, India, 2007

skills and attitude to work hard and compete, to become a leader in the industry.

He completed his degree from Stanford University in 2001.[12] The year varies with sources. Multiple reports state the year to be 1999 or 2000. An article in *Mint* stated, 'In what can be described as his tenacity and a hallmark of his greatness, Premji completed his Bachelor of Science degree in electrical engineering from Stanford thirty-four years later in 2000.'[13]

In a television interview, Premji recalled his early days after he had taken over and the doubts that a shareholder had expressed on his abilities at that time. The shareholder, in Premji's first meeting at the helm of (now) Wipro, had suggested that Premji step down and let professional managers run the company.[14] The shareholder's comments had a deep effect on him and made him determined to prove the person wrong. Premji had no prior experience in running a company, and the only strength that he recalled having was his ability to work hard.

The next twenty years were a whirlwind of activity when Premji diversified from Wipro's main business of Sunflower

---

[12]Harichandan Arakali, 'Holding Wealth, the Azim Premji Way', *Forbes India*, 9 December 2016, accessed 30 June 2019, http://www.forbesindia.com/article/india-rich-list-2016/holding-wealth-the-azim-premji-way/45077/1

[13]Harish Puppala and Rakesh Sharma, 'Digging Deeper—Azim Premji: The End of an Era', Moneycontrol.com, accessed 30 June 2019, https://www.moneycontrol.com/news/podcast/digging-deeper-azim-premji-the-end-of-an-era-4090341.html

[14]Bloomberg Billionaires Index, accessed 4 September 2019, https://www.bloomberg.com/billionaires/profiles/azim-h-premji/

Vanaspati oil to soaps, and other consumer care products, and then to other businesses including Information Technology (IT) products, engineering services, medical equipment solutions and Fast-Moving Consumer Goods (FMCG).[15]

His wife Yasmeen stated that besides the virtues of his persistence, what helped was his ability to focus and work with determination towards achieving his goal.[16] At the time, the family owned about 50 per cent stake in Wipro, but Premji had been using his dividends income to buy back shares in Wipro. By 2000, he had accumulated more than 75 per cent of shares in Wipro. This shareholding pushed him to the league of the richest Indian, valuing his wealth to be $30 billion.[17]

By 2002, Premji held nearly 84 per cent of the shares, from the 50 per cent that he had held when he joined the company in 1966 as the managing director. However, the market regulators put a cap on the promoter holding on to 75 per cent, and consequently, he was forced to bring down his ownership to that level.[18]

The first opportunity to diversify came his way in 1977, when the Government of India clamped down on multinationals, leading to the departure of global giants such

---

[15] Rukmini Rao, 'The Visionary', *Business Today*, 19 March 2019, accessed 1 June 2019, https://www.businesstoday.in/magazine/best-ceos-2019/the-visionary/story/318667.html
[16] Ibid.
[17] Varun Sood and Sundeep Khanna, 'Making of Azim Premji: The Philanthropist', *Livemint*, 24 June 2019, accessed 28 June 2019, https://www.livemint.com/companies/people/making-of-azim-premji-the-philanthropist-1561390035003.html
[18] Ibid.

as International Business Machines (IBM) and The Coca-Cola Company from India. Wipro, under Premji, stepped in to fill that gap and began manufacturing computers and other electronic products.[19]

The IT products soon made way for customized software services when the markets opened up, and imports became much easier.

Later, as it moved up the value chain, Wipro moved into Research & Development (R&D) and design services, to offer higher-margin products to customers, thus moving away from the commoditized products.

Today, Wipro comprises two entities. The first is the leading IT major, Wipro Limited, which is in IT, business process services, and consulting. The second is the demerged (in 2013) non-IT products entity, the closely held Wipro Enterprises (P) Limited, which comprises two main businesses, namely, Wipro Consumer Care & Lighting, primarily into personal care products, lighting solutions and office furniture, and Wipro Infrastructure Engineering, which provides hydraulic solutions for a wide range of applications including aerospace and defence and complete end-to-end solutions in water and wastewater treatment for industrial applications.[20] This company also has two joint ventures, one with General Electric (GE) for medical equipment, and another with Japan's Kawasaki for precision machinery.[21] Around December 2012, Wipro sold off its oldest

---

[19]Yaroslav Trofimov, 'How a Muslim Billionaire Thrives in Hindu India', *The Wall Street Journal*, 11 September 2007, accessed 29 June 2019, https://www.wsj.com/articles/SB118947228823323260

[20]Annual reports 2017–2018 and website of Wipro

[21]Harichandan Arakali, 'Holding Wealth, the Azim Premji Way', *Forbes*

brand, Sunflower Vanaspati, to Cargill, Inc., the US-based food processing company, for an undisclosed amount.

In 2009, Premji was awarded an honorary doctorate from Wesleyan University in Middletown, Connecticut, and in 2015, Mysore University conferred him with an honorary doctorate.

In 2005, he was awarded the Padma Bhushan for his outstanding contribution to trade and commerce by the Government of India. In 2011, he was awarded the Padma Vibhushan, the second-highest civilian award conferred by the Government of India.[22]

In June 2019, after more than fifty years at the helm of Wipro, Azim Premji announced that he was stepping down as chairman and managing director of Wipro Ltd. Premji also announced that he was stepping down in favour of his son Rishad. This was not a spontaneous or a knee-jerk reaction, but the culmination of a long and well-thought-out process that had started more than ten years ago, since Rishad joined the leadership team in 2007.[23] Rishad would take over as

---

India, 9 December 2016, accessed 30 June 2019, http://www.forbesindia.com/article/india-rich-list-2016/holding-wealth-the-azim-premji-way/45077/1

[22]'Happy Birthday Azim Premji! Did You Know These Five Facts About the Wipro Chairman?', accessed 30 June 2019, https://www.timesnownews.com/business-economy/companies/article/happy-birthday-azim-premji-did-you-know-these-five-facts-about-wipro-chairman/258930

[23]Shilpa Phadnis, 'Rishad Premji Has Very Big Shoes to Fill at Wipro', *The Economic Times*, 7 June 2019, accessed 30 June 2019, https://economictimes.indiatimes.com/tech/internet/rishad-premji-has-very-big-shoes-to-fill-atwipro/articleshow/69685945.cms?utm_source=newsletter&utm_medium=email&utm_campaign=Dailynewsletter&ncode=047e0d7f8dbf407d50faffd920c58bc6

executive chairman, and the company Chief Electoral Officer (CEO) Abidali Z. Neemuchwala, would succeed him as managing director.

Rishad has a MBA business degree from the Harvard Business School and has been working on various projects at Wipro ever since he joined as a business manager, treasury and investor relations, in 2007.[24] This position had given him a broad exposure to the consulting, finance, treasury and operations of the organization. In September 2010, he took over the position of chief strategy officer of the IT services, reporting to the then joint CEOs of Wipro.

Tariq, Premji's younger son, has different accomplishments from Rishad. Tariq has been working at the Azim Premji Foundation since 2012. He studied at Mumbai's St Mary's School and has a degree in commerce from St Joseph's College, Bengaluru. Before joining PremjiInvest, the family office of Azim Premji, Tariq worked at a BPO firm for nearly a year. In 2018, Tariq was appointed to the Board of Wipro Enterprises, the $1.23 billion privately held non-IT business that makes soaps such as Santoor and builds aerospace sub-systems for plane makers such as Airbus and Boeing.[25]

---

[24]Rukmini Rao, '"Son" Rise at Wipro: Tech Major Announces Change of Guard As Rishad Premji Appointed New Executive Chairman', *Business Today*, 14 June 2019, accessed 25 August 2019, https://www.businesstoday.in/current/corporate/son-rise-at-wipro-announces-change-of-guard-azim-premji-steps-down-rishad-premji/story/354242.html

[25]'Azim Premji and Sons Ltd: Tariq Appointed to the Board of Wipro Enterprises', *The Economic Times*, 8 June 2018, accessed 30 June 2019, https://economictimes.indiatimes.com/news/company/corporate-trends/azim-premji-and-sons-ltd-tariq-appointed-to-the-board-of-

Rishad has been trained well to step into Azim Premji's shoes at Wipro—big shoes, undoubtedly—but being filled in by someone who has been trained under Premji's watchful eyes over the last ten years. It is interesting to note that while Azim Premji has handed over the reins to Rishad, a small but very significant exception is that Premji has left Rishad and Tariq to create their own wealth, since a large part of his wealth has already been given to his philanthropic foundations.[26]

Let us study the person in greater detail to understand the man behind the headlines. Though one must admit that these (the headlines) are also very few in comparison to other business moguls, as the reticent and media-shy Premji would rather go about his work than devote any time to enhancing his media presence! He is known to get upset if there are any reports in the media covering him. He wonders what the fuss is about, and if there should be media reports. In spite of this, let us use the limited information available to learn from this reticent billionaire.

---

wipro-enterprises/articleshow/64508056.cms

[26] 'Azim Premji's Lasting Legacy Is of Munificent Money', *Financial Express*, 8 June 2019, accessed 30 June 2019, https://www.financialexpress.com/opinion/azim-premjis-lasting-legacy-is-of-munificent-money/1601160/

1
AZIM PREMJI: THE PERSON
BE DETAIL-ORIENTED, AND HUMBLE

He has no ego. He is the most organized, structured and detail-oriented person I have known, and is willing to learn from people across all levels, both within and outside the organization.[1]

—Rishad Premji, Azim Premji's elder son

The Wipro website mentions the following about Azim Premji. This has been quoted here.[2]

---

[1] Harichandan Arakali, 'Holding Wealth, the Azim Premji Way', *Forbes India*, 9 December 2016, accessed 30 June 2019, http://www.forbesindia.com/article/india-rich-list-2016/holding-wealth-the-azim-premji-way/45077/1

[2] Wipro.com, accessed 20 June 2019, https://www.wipro.com/en-IN/leadership/azim-h-premji/

Over the years, Azim Premji has received numerous honours and accolades, which he considers as recognition for the team of Wipro and the Foundation. *Business Week* listed him amongst the top 30 entrepreneurs in world history. *Financial Times, Time, Fortune* and *Forbes* have all named him as of one the most influential people in the world, citing his leadership in business and philanthropy, including the contributions to improving public education. *The Journal of Foreign Policy* has listed him amongst the top global thinkers. *The Economic Times* bestowed Mr Premji with the Lifetime Achievement Award.

Premji is the first Indian recipient of the Faraday Medal and has been conferred honorary doctorates by the Michigan State University and Wesleyan University (in the US), and the Indian Institutes of Technology at Bombay, Roorkee and Kharagpur, amongst others. The Republic of France has conferred upon him their highest civilian award, 'Knight of the Legion of Honor'. He was conferred in January 2011 with the Padma Vibhushan, the second-highest civilian award in India. The Carnegie Medal of Philanthropy was bestowed on him in 2017, hailing the 'conscience, integrity and compassion that have guided his visionary giving ... (with) invaluable benefit to both, that nation and to the world.

MODESTY AND HUMILITY

In spite of these achievements, Premji is known to be very

humble and low-key. When he announced his departure in June 2019, he wrote an email to Wipro's employees. The major part of the letter consisted of introducing the new chairman and the new managing director. He thought it fit not to mention his name or his achievements except for an understated line at the bottom of the letter. This was very surprising, especially when he has many significant achievements to talk about.[3]

SIMPLE LIVING, HIGH THINKING

Premji's penchant to avoid the media and public attention is a trait that is characteristic of very few other industrialists. He goes out of his way to avoid the glare of the media spotlight and continues doing his work silently. As we will see in the next section, this trait, coupled with his simplicity and frugal behaviour, has been his hallmark.

Another report states that he was very embarrassed when he found his name on top of the *Forbes* list of Indian billionaires, which continued for a few years, from 2000 onwards.[4] He would have preferred to remain away from the spotlight, which was now focused on him. This was the kind

---

[3] Aakar Patel, 'Azim Premji to Hang Up His Boots: Wipro Chairman Led a Modest Life, Set Example for Other Billionaires to Give up Surplus Wealth', Firstpost.com, 10 June 2019, accessed 29 June 2019, https://www.firstpost.com/business/azim-premji-to-hang-up-his-boots-wipro-chairman-led-a-modest-life-set-example-for-other-billionaires-to-give-up-surplus-wealth-6783971.html

[4] 'Opinion: The Blazer of Diverse Trials to a Greater Goal', *Livemint*, 9 June 2019, https://www.livemint.com/opinion/online-views/opinion-the-blazer-of-diverse-trails-to-a-greater-goal-1560104111223.html

of attention he did not like.

In a newspaper article, Suresh Senapaty, his chief financial officer (CFO) who stepped down in 2015, had stated[5] that simplicity was an integral part of Premji's DNA, which had remained unchanged for a long time, since the day he first met him. Premji embodied simple living and high thinking.

ATTENTION TO DETAIL

People around him say that Premji is a very detailed-oriented person, who plans and thinks out his every move. He plans meticulously and is known not to take any impulsive steps. As a result of this detailed planning, his calendar is filled up months in advance.

Another anecdote related by Premji's team members stated something that we shall see in detail, in a subsequent chapter—his philanthropic endeavours. Premji is not only a good businessman but also a smart philanthropist. His efforts in philanthropy have also been subject to the same careful analysis and deep thought that his business received. Premji had researched for more than a year, trying to figure out where he could make an impact with his philanthropy. He identified education, since he believed in the adage, 'Give a man a fish and you feed him for a day; teach a man to fish and you feed him for a lifetime!'

---

[5]Suresh Senapaty, 'Opinion: Azim Premji, the Embodiment of Simple Living and High Thinking', *Livemint*, 9 April 2019, accessed 30 June 2019, https://www.livemint.com/opinion/columns/opinion-azim-premji-the-embodiment-of-simple-living-and-high-thinking-1554499738628.html

Premji focused specifically on primary education and government schools to avoid duplication of effort. These are institutions which impact the lives of the largest number of children, but all his efforts are carried out without publicity or using his name.[6]

One of his team members, Ashok Soota,[7] related the story of how Premji had hired him in 1984. Soota was interviewing for the position of president of the IT business. Their interactions were held over several days, and Soota was impressed with the detail and depth that Premji went into while hiring. Premji also met the references given by Soota. He was aware that he absolutely had to make the right call, as he was making an important decision.[8] Premji was also known to take detailed notes while discussing anything, as he did while calling up the references. He was firm in his belief of hiring the right person and then empowering him.

FOCUSED APPROACH

Premji believed in being focused on the responsibility at hand and giving it his fullest attention. He was so focused on what

---

[6] Suresh Senapaty, 'Opinion: Azim Premji, the Embodiment of Simple Living and High Thinking', *Livemint*, 9 April 2019, accessed 30 June 2019, https://www.livemint.com/opinion/columns/opinion-azim-premji-the-embodiment-of-simple-living-and-high-thinking-1554499738628.html

[7] Ashok Soota served as president of Wipro Infotech from 1984 to 1999.

[8] Raghu Krishnan, 'Azim Premji's Strength Is the People He Picks: Ashok Soota', *The Economic Times*, 7 June 2019, accessed 30 June 2019, https://economictimes.indiatimes.com/tech/ites/azim-premjis-strength-is-the-people-he-picks-ashok-soota/articleshow/69684052.cms

he was doing that he did not take on any other work, even other Board memberships, while heading Wipro. When asked about this, he stated that he preferred to do so, as he believed that he needed to focus on his business and this would need all his attention.[9] He believed that he could contribute to Wipro and make it successful, and he concentrated on doing exactly that. Can you imagine stronger work ethics?

Premji relates an incident[10] where he was criticized at the large shareholding that he had accumulated. As mentioned earlier, he had started with the family shareholding of 50 per cent and had used all his dividends to buy back Wipro stock. This led to a situation where, at one time, he held about 85 per cent of Wipro stock. He was questioned for retaining such a large stake in Wipro, a company that was doing well. His answer was, 'I don't want somebody coming and hampering growth.'[11] On another occasion, while discussing his stock-buying practice from dividends, he had justified the step, stating that it showed his confidence in the firm. If *he* was not confident of the company's performance, then who would be, he asked?

---

[9]Varun Sood and Sundeep Khanna, 'Making of Azim Premji: The Philanthropist', *Livemint*, 24 June 2019, accessed 28 June 2019, https://www.livemint.com/companies/people/making-of-azim-premji-the-philanthropist-1561390035003.html

[10]ET Bureau, 'Azim Premji to Retire As Executive Chairman of Wipro, Son Rishad to Take Over', *The Economic Times*, 7 June 2019, accessed 30 June 2019, https://economictimes.indiatimes.com/tech/ites/azim-premji-to-retire-from-wirpo-on-july-30/articleshow/69675970.cms

[11]Ibid.

LEARNINGS

The instances mentioned above show Premji's dedication and professionalism in focusing on the task at hand while additionally ensuring that he has adequate time to focus on his work. Usually, leaders take on multiple responsibilities and obligations. They may be great at multitasking or may need to do so due to reasons such as influencing policy, industry lobbying, social or media presence or support for causes of interest, to mention a few reasons. And these positions of responsibility could be prestigious or powerful. But the challenge is that these could be a source of distraction to the main business, or the business could suffer if the leader is preoccupied with other pursuits. One has seen multiple cases where businesses have suffered due to the promoters not devoting enough time to the business. Thus, not only does the business lose out, but the shareholders, investors and employees also suffer. This happens even when the promoters are busy raising funds, fighting cases of litigation against the company or pursuing other interests or hobbies.

Premji's single-minded focus on the business helped him avoid such distractions due to his preference to devote all his attention and energies to growing the business. Such focus is usually rare for industrialists who have various demands on their time and energies. But one clear reason for his success is his preference to remain focused on his work. It is instructive to note that after stepping down from the top job at Wipro, which is on the trajectory to fast growth, he remains focused on his second passion—his philanthropic interests.

Premji's humility is also worth devoting some attention

to. According to Clayton M. Christensen, a professor at the Harvard Business School, the one characteristic of all humble people is their high level of self-esteem. This is backed by self-awareness of who they are, and feeling good about themselves. It is this act of feeling good about oneself that requires one to be humble. Thus, humble people want to help others and feel good about themselves. He goes on to state that the lack of self-esteem causes people to behave abusively, arrogantly or in a demeaning manner towards others. Thus, putting someone else down causes these people to feel good about themselves.[12] This could be an excellent diagnostic method for future leaders to examine their behaviour and pursue humility. After all, true learning only takes place when we have the attitude that we can learn something from everyone.

On a different note, I would like to cite an example from the *Ramayana*.[13] After Lord Ram vanquishes Ravan in battle, Lord Ram turns to his younger brother Laxman and instructs him to go and learn the art of administration from Ravan, a great and learned scholar. The greatness in Lord Ram was in recognizing the fact that there was something that they could learn even from the enemy! The story goes that Laxman went and asked Ravan to teach him, whilst he stood near Ravan's head. When Ravan did not acknowledge him, Laxman went back to Lord Ram, and that is when Ram told him that if one

---

[12] Clayton M. Christensen, 'How Will You Measure Your Life?', *Harvard Business Review*, pg. 46–51, July–August 2010

[13] Ajeet, 'What Did Lakshman Learn from Ravana?', Speakingtree.in, 15 June 2016, accessed 1 July 2019, https://www.speakingtree.in/blog/what-did-lakshman-learn-from-ravana

has to learn something from anyone, then one has to stand not near his head, but at his feet. Laxman went to Ravan again and stood at his feet. Ravan then imparted his learnings to Laxman.

This is another thought-provoking instance of how leaders should be humble enough to learn from all possible opportunities. Premji's humility serves as a reminder of how great industrialists remain humble to recognize and seize all learning opportunities.

2
FRUGALITY

In 2018, *Forbes* magazine had ranked Azim Premji as second in the list of billionaires in India.[14] He was also ranked 36th in the world by the same magazine. He is reputed to be extremely frugal. In spite of his wealth, Premji still flies economy class, avoids costly cars and ostentatious displays of wealth.[15]

Premji is also known to avoid even the appearance of spending lavishly. He has been reported to have refused to accept an upgrade to first class even when the airline offered it. He stated, 'It's a philosophy. I apply the same standard for

---

[14]*Forbes* billionaires list, accessed 8 July 2019, https://www.forbes.com/profile/azim-premji/#48ac9ff57924

[15]Kalpana Pathak, 'Azim Premji Raises Philanthropy Bar with $21 Billion Total Pledge', *Livemint*, 13 March 2019, accessed 30 June 2019, https://www.livemint.com/companies/people/azim-premji-raises-philanthropy-bar-with-21-billion-total-pledge-1552500208294.html

myself, as I do for everybody in the organization'.[16]

Premji's explanation for the thought behind his frugality is that his efforts were towards building a culture in his organization. If this culture was prevalent, the employees would be careful with the company money. They would spend the company money with the same amount of care as they would if they were spending their own money. And this would start with the leaders, who would be responsible for setting these rules, who would need to follow these rules themselves, to set an example first.[17]

A Wipro Annual General Meeting in Bengaluru's Electronic City was held at a large and basic meeting venue. It did not have any frills that would be the hallmark of any other fancier venues used by other companies. Premji was questioned by a shareholder on his choice of venue and why he had not chosen a fancier one. Premji is reported to having said, 'I have been a scrooge for seventy years, can't change now'.[18]

Premji also reportedly monitored the amount of toilet paper rolls consumed by Wipro employees. Wipro employees at Sarjapur, Bengaluru, Wipro's headquarters, related stories of them bumping into Premji, whom they met during their travels, while he was also travelling economy class.

He used to also walk around the campus in the evenings to check whether the lights were switched off after working

---

[16]Steve Hamm, *Bangalore Tiger, How Indian Tech Upstart Wipro Is Rewriting the Rules of Global Competition*, pg. 128, Tata McGraw-Hill, India, 2007.
[17]Ibid.
[18]Pankaj Mishra, 'Hello, Azim Seth!', Factordaily.com, blog, 22 July 2016, accessed 29 June 2019, https://factordaily.com/hello-azim-seth/

hours and used to regularly ask people to switch off the lights.[19]

His personal preferences are legendary and the subject of much admiration. The story may be apocryphal, of his monitoring the toilet paper usage in the Wipro offices, as I have not managed to find an authentic source for this story. But since this has been mentioned everywhere, I suspect, as someone had stated, that even an untruth, if repeated quite frequently, is regarded as the truth!

But there are other examples of his frugality and wanting to cut costs or wasteful expenditure, besides his encouraging employees to switch the lights off before leaving the office. He is also known to have not changed his car, having used the same Ford Escort for eight years, before changing to a Toyota Corolla.[20] (As for his choice of cars, another article mentioned that he had traded his car for a second-hand Mercedes which he is said to have bought from one of his employees.)[21]

He is also stated to have often taken an autorickshaw from the airport to the Wipro offices.[22] He is also not averse to

---

[19]Radhika Dhawad, 'By Donating Rs 52,750 Crore, Azim Premji Becomes Most Generous Indian Ever', Nationnext.in, accessed 29 June 2019, https://nationnext.in/azim-premji-most-generous-indian-ever/

[20]Pankaj Mishra, 'Hello, Azim Seth!', Factordaily.com, blog, 22 July 2016, accessed 29 June 2019, https://factordaily.com/hello-azim-seth/

[21]'Indian Billionaire Drops Honda City, Drives Secondhand Mercedes', *Siliconindia*, 30 June 2014, accessed 30 June 2019, https://www.siliconindia.com/news/business/Indian-Billionaire-Drops-Honda-City-Drives-Secondhand-Mercedes-nid-168684-cid-3.html

[22]'Meet 5 Geek Gods Who Choose to Live a Simple Life', *The Economic Times*, 4 February 2015, accessed 29 June 2019, https://economictimes.indiatimes.com/people/meet-5-geek-gods-who-choose-to-live-a-simple-

taking a ride on a public bus. The fact that he walked the 250 metres from his home to the Wipro offices, situated on a five-hectare campus, could explain his hesitation to buy a car! This would also explain his preference to walk to work every day.

He is also known to, besides travelling in economy class, stay in budget hotels or company guest houses, eating at the company canteen, and wearing non-branded suits. Another instance relates to his having paper plates at a lunch function organized during his son Rishad's wedding.[23]

He expects his employees to be watchful about saving money wherever possible. He says, 'What is good for my employees is good for me.'[24] And eventually, every penny saved is a penny earned, for philanthropy.[25]

Another Wipro executive recalls that once, Premji sent out emails first thing in the morning pointing out how fax paper could be saved by using alternative communication methods.[26]

One of his executives said this about Premji, 'He's (Premji) a humble guy. He doesn't put himself above everybody. He

---

life/azim-premji-chairman-wipro/slideshow/46141104.cms

[23]Sarojam, 'Azim Premji', Speakingtree.in, blog, accessed 30 June 2019, https://www.speakingtree.in/blog/azim-premji-465754

[24]Pankaj Mishra, 'Hello, Azim Seth!', Factordaily.com, blog, 22 July 2016, accessed 29 June 2019, https://factordaily.com/hello-azim-seth/

[25]Harichandan Arakali, 'Holding Wealth, the Azim Premji Way', *Forbes India*, 9 December 2016, accessed 30 June 2019, http://www.forbesindia.com/article/india-rich-list-2016/holding-wealth-the-azim-premji-way/45077/1

[26]Steve Hamm, *Bangalore Tiger, How Indian Tech Upstart Wipro Is Rewriting the Rules of Global Competition*, Tata McGraw-Hill, India, 2007

works as hard if not harder than anybody else. Other CEOs act like they want to be treated like royalty. He's not like that.'[27]

Rana Kapoor, formerly Yes Bank chairman and CEO at the time, recalled a meeting with Premji at Yes Bank's Worli offices in Mumbai. The meeting dragged on till lunchtime, and he recalls that when asked for lunch options, Premji suggested that they order burgers and milkshakes from a fast food outlet which was just below their building. And that day, that was exactly what they had for lunch—burgers and strawberry shake.[28]

Premji's preference for simplicity extended to his fondness for street food. During his global travels, as a part of his roadshow for the New York Stock Exchange listing in 2000, Premji was said to be at ease, stopping for a meal of crabs on the streets of Singapore, or in Mumbai at the offices of Morgan Stanley, where he expressed his preference for vada pav for lunch.[29]

The above incident demonstrates a clear case of preferring 'functionality over ornamentation'.[30]

He leads a simple life filled with austerity and hard work.

---

[27] Rick Garnick, former head of North American Operations, Wipro, quoted from Steve Hamm, *Bangalore Tiger, How Indian Tech Upstart Wipro is Rewriting the Rules of Global Competition*, pg. 104, Tata McGraw-Hill India, 2007

[28] Pankaj Mishra, 'Hello, Azim Seth!', Factordaily.com, blog, 22 July 2016, accessed 29 June 2019, https://factordaily.com/hello-azim-seth/

[29] Suresh Senapaty, 'Opinion: Azim Premji, the Embodiment of Simple Living and High Thinking', *Livemint*, 9 April 2019, accessed 30 June 2019, https://www.livemint.com/opinion/columns/opinion-azim-premji-the-embodiment-of-simple-living-and-high-thinking-1554499738628.html

[30] Ibid.

He reportedly wakes up every day at 4.30 a.m. and then shoots off various emails to his company managers across four continents while having his morning coffee.[31] While he encourages and pushes his managers to save costs, he might not hesitate to make a $100 million investment in Wipro, if needed. His thought towards wealth has been that he is a trustee of his wealth, not the owner, and this mindset has influenced his actions.[32]

LEARNINGS

Premji's most admirable attribute is perhaps his frugality. This is even more surprising given that the wealth that he has created ranks him amongst the top three billionaires in India and amongst the top 50 billionaires globally. So, it is not a question of not being able to afford these expenses. But the frugality and simplicity come from a basic nature to avoid wasteful expenditure as a conscious choice.

And it is this choice that one needs to appreciate. As a family business consultant, I have seen many wealthy families where the family has not bothered to keep track of their expenses or prefer to spend ostentatiously, just because they can. Oftentimes, this has led to disastrous results. Similarly,

---

[31] 'India's Tech King', *Bloomberg Businessweek*, 13 October 2003, accessed 29 June 2019, https://www.bloomberg.com/news/articles/2003-10-12/indias-tech-king

[32] Harichandan Arakali, 'Holding Wealth, the Azim Premji Way', *Forbes India*, 9 December 2016, accessed 30 June 2019, http://www.forbesindia.com/article/india-rich-list-2016/holding-wealth-the-azim-premji-way/45077/1

even in companies, the amount of carelessness in spending leads to profligate spending. This leads to these companies or families being able to manage when the times are good, but the challenges arise when the good times go away. And that's when the problems begin. Premji's tendency to watch every expense carefully shows that he had been concerned about this aspect. His constant watch over expenditure made the others also cost-conscious, a habit that they did appreciate even years after leaving Wipro.

On a lighter note, one can also point out that the fact that Azim Premji owned more than 84 per cent of the company gave him another reason to be personally invested! But regardless of the ownership pattern, his subsequently giving away almost 67 per cent of holdings to charity also drives him and the organization, because now the mindset is that they are creating wealth for doing good in society. This is not just for the enrichment of any individual shareholder or promoter families. This way, even his people and stakeholders would not mind the frugality being followed by the organization, and working hard, since the profits would be, eventually, for philanthropy.

This is almost similar to another reputed business family, the Tatas, where the trusts own around 66 per cent of Tata Sons and use the profits and dividends for charitable avenues.[33] Since this is adequately covered in my previous book, I will not repeat this in detail here.

Premji kept donating his wealth but no one was aware of the extent of his generosity. Premji was driven by the desire to

---

[33]Rajiv Agarwal, *Succeed to Inspire Like the Tatas*, Rupa Publications, 2019

create wealth, cut costs, and increase margins and profits, so that the contribution to philanthropy would get enhanced. A few years later, when he gave away a large part of his wealth, all his detractors were silenced, and no one pointed any fingers at Premji for creating and accumulating such a large amount of wealth! This magnitude of philanthropy was unprecedented anywhere else in the world.

On a different note, the frugality and simplicity come from an inherent desire to lead a simple life. Premji was frugal and not afraid to enforce it. This virtue needs courage to stand up to, and not be influenced by others or be subjected to the peer pressure of adhering to what others may be doing. This is possible only when one has a very strong sense of self-confidence and conviction of one's actions.

The other school of thought is that Wipro did not have an alternative to being frugal, as, at the time, the company was just finding its feet in a new IT market. And it did not have the funds to survive. One of the first employees, who had been sent to the US to scope out business, remembers staying in low-budget conditions and sharing rooms to cut costs.

Steve Hamm in his book on Wipro, titled *Bangalore Tiger*, mentions that in the early days of Wipro, foreign exchange controls prevented large expenses on overseas travel. This resulted in the executives being forced to travel economy class for the twenty-hour journeys to the US from Bengaluru. Engineers and programme managers working from the client offices used to occupy hotel rooms on a double or triple share basis. Inexpensive apartments were rented out for longer-term projects lasting for months or years. The policies have been relaxed a little, but the frugal culture is so deeply ingrained that some of the practices continue. Premji explained, 'I don't think we do anything extreme now. Because of globalization, we have gone more liberal on it, but we still value money.'[34]

The learning from this is that when the culture to save or cut unnecessary costs becomes deeply ingrained, self-regulation and monitoring becomes a habit. So, additional policing may not always be needed.

What is also admirable is Premji's simplicity when it comes to his lifestyle and personal habits. At a time when one reads about huge displays of wealth, his low-key lifestyle appears as a refreshing exception. What is also more pertinent to note is that Premji deserves due recognition and praise, because all the wealth has been created by him. True, he did inherit the family business from his father, but the amount of growth that he created and the value of it now is far greater compared to what he had inherited.

His core characteristics of frugality, hard work and simplicity were the differentiating factors that made Premji an example to emulate. The simple fact that he continued to work as hard as he always did, even when his company Wipro did exceedingly well, and created huge wealth for all its stakeholders, was admirable and worth emulating.

---

[34]Steve Hamm, *Bangalore Tiger, How Indian Tech Upstart Wipro is Rewriting the Rules of Global Competition*, pg. 129, Tata McGraw-Hill, India, 2007

3
INTEGRITY AND CORPORATE GOVERNANCE

Azim Premji is regarded as one of the few promoters who was uncompromising in integrity and maintained a very high level of corporate governance. One of his team members at Wipro is stated to have said that Premji considered himself as a fiduciary custodian of the wealth. This is in spite of the fact that Premji had started to give away a substantial part of his wealth for social welfare purposes.[35]

An anecdote that is often stated is that of Premji refusing to allow his son Rishad to use the company guest house in London in 2005. His son was then working for Bain & Company, a well-known consulting firm in the UK. The rationale that was given by Premji was that Rishad was not

---

[35]Harichandan Arakali, 'Holding Wealth, the Azim Premji Way', *Forbes India*, 9 December 2016, accessed 30 June 2019, http://www.forbesindia.com/article/india-rich-list-2016/holding-wealth-the-azim-premji-way/45077/1

a Wipro employee at the time and hence was not entitled to use the company property![36]

Integrity is something that Azim Premji has always treated as a non-negotiable attribute. There are ample stories of his reluctance to compromise on this principle.

A story recalled by an ex-employee of Wipro was one where Premji instructed a Wipro factory to be run using diesel generators for generating power. This was because the factory had not got its power connection, and the electric line to the factory still had to be laid down. The then minister wanted a bribe just to approve the permission for laying down a power line to the factory! Readers can understand that although this must have been a more troublesome and expensive option, Premji was not willing to pay the bribe. This was, however, a short-term decision, as eighteen months later, the minister's party was voted out in the elections, and the company was connected to the main power grid.[37] Premji was willing to compromise on his efforts for lowering costs, but would not agree to pay a bribe!

Another example is related by Premji[38] where the company took its non-negotiable stand on business ethics. There was a Wipro employee who had travelled from Chennai to Mumbai by train. Even though the employee was entitled to travel on a

---

[36]Harichandan Arakali, 'Holding Wealth, the Azim Premji Way', *Forbes India*, 9 December 2016, accessed 30 June 2019, http://www.forbesindia.com/article/india-rich-list-2016/holding-wealth-the-azim-premji-way/45077/1

[37]Pankaj Mishra, 'Hello, Azim Seth!', Factordaily.com, blog, 22 July 2016, accessed 29 June 2019, https://factordaily.com/hello-azim-seth/

[38]Steve Hamm, *Bangalore Tiger, How Indian Tech Upstart Wipro is Rewriting the Rules of Global Competition*, pg. 73, Tata McGraw-Hill, India, 2007

first-class ticket, they travelled on a second-class ticket. When the time came to claim the expenses from the company, the employee filed a claim for the first-class fare and pocketed the difference. The company discovered the truth and fired the employee for this action. The employee was a member of the labour union and took up the matter with the union. The union protested on his behalf and insisted that the employee be taken back. The company refused. This refusal prompted the union to go on strike which lasted for three months. Azim Premji did not back down, and stuck to his guns about enforcing integrity. He stated, 'At Wipro, there are no exceptions. And there is no price you are not willing to pay, for doing the right thing'.[39]

Another incident, which is often quoted, relates to the time that Premji was travelling from Bengaluru to Delhi. He had booked a ticket in the economy class, as he always did. However, that one time, he was travelling by Kingfisher Airlines, which was a new airline at the time. The fact that Premji was travelling by Kingfisher Airlines was a big event for the airline, even if it was in the economy class. So, Kingfisher upgraded him to first class as a courtesy. Premji refused the upgrade offer. He was under the mistaken impression that it was an executive of his company who was responsible for the upgrade (she wasn't) and reprimanded her. This stemmed from his belief that the company's money belonged to the shareholders and needed to be spent wisely.[40]

---

[39] Steve Hamm, *Bangalore Tiger, How Indian Tech Upstart Wipro is Rewriting the Rules of Global Competition*, pg. 73, Tata McGraw-Hill, India, 2007
[40] Varun Sood and Sundeep Khanna, 'Making of Azim Premji: The

'As a promoter, he has been uncompromising on integrity and has maintained the highest degree of corporate governance,' says Senapaty. 'He feels personally responsible for the fiduciary custodianship of wealth, a substantial portion of which is set aside for social purposes.'[41]

This is perhaps one of the reasons why Wipro has been appearing on the World's Most Ethical Companies' honorees list for the last eight years running, including in 2019.[42] This list is released annually by Ethisphere Institute which 'honours those companies who recognise their critical role to influence and drive positive change in the business community and societies around the world and work to maximize their impact wherever possible.'[43] This is no small achievement, since Wipro was only one of the two companies from India on the list for 2019. The other was Tata Steel.

According to their website,[44] The World's Most Ethical Companies assessment is based upon the Ethisphere

---

Philanthropist', *Livemint*, 24 June 2019, accessed 28 June 2019, https://www.livemint.com/companies/people/making-of-azim-premji-the-philanthropist-1561390035003.html

[41] Harichandan Arakali, 'Holding Wealth, the Azim Premji Way', *Forbes India*, 9 December 2016, accessed 30 June 2019, http://www.forbesindia.com/article/india-rich-list-2016/holding-wealth-the-azim-premji-way/45077/1

[42] Wipro.com, accessed 30 June 2019, https://www.wipro.com/newsroom/press-releases/2019/wipro-ranked-third-fastest-growing-global-it-services-brand-in-2019/

[43] Ethisphere.com, accessed 30 June 2019, https://ethisphere.com/2018-worlds-most-ethical-companies/

[44] ANI, 'Wipro Named World's Most Ethical Firm 2015', *Business Today*, 9 March 2015, accessed 30 June 2019, https://www.businesstoday.in/current/corporate/wipro-named-world-most-ethical-firm-2015/story/216703.html

Institute's Ethics Quotient™ (EQ) framework to provide a means to objectively assess an organization's performance.

Information is collected to provide a comprehensive sampling of criteria of core competencies and not just all aspects of corporate governance, risk, sustainability, compliance and ethics. The EQ framework and methodology is determined by an internal network of thought leaders and an advisory panel.

There are five key categories for the score: ethics and compliance programme (35 per cent), corporate citizenship and responsibility (20 per cent), culture of ethics (20 per cent), governance (15 per cent) and leadership, innovation and reputation (10 per cent).

LEARNINGS

This is a more detailed section, as there are multiple aspects that are discussed.

FIDUCIARY CUSTODIAN

Let us understand what a fiduciary custodian does. As a fiduciary custodian, the primary responsibility of a person would be to ensure that the wealth is preserved and passed on to the next generation. This means that the wealth should not be destroyed during the time it is in your care. Most wealth creators and their successors consume the wealth during their lifetimes and hence the next generation may find that there is very little wealth that is passed on. This is also the essence of the saying for business families, 'From shirtsleeves to shirtsleeves, in three generations', or that wealth does not last more than three generations. That is, one generation creates the wealth, the second maintains it and the third destroys it. This has been seen in the case of most multiple wealthy families all around the world, including India. There is another well-known statistic which says that only 4 per cent of the families manage to survive until the fourth generation!

Let us understand fiduciary custody in terms of a wealthy family that has inherited a huge amount of wealth. In this case, fiduciary custody comes with the awareness that the wealth is not one's property, one can't do with it as one deems fit, nor spend it in any manner that one desires. It means that the inheritors can use the wealth for their well-being, sustenance, education or for building up the family business. But this does not mean that they can be extravagant or take unnecessary risks which could destroy the wealth. Hence, they have to act as preservers and grow the wealth, which is entrusted to them, and which is under their responsibility.

Premji has stated that he is in such a role. We saw this from the later part of his life, when he passed on his wealth to his philanthropic trust. Hence, when he acts frugally in Wipro, or in his lifestyle choices, he is, in a way, saving money to ensure that there is more money saved up to give for social causes! This is a trait that one cannot find fault with, but only appreciate. Also, he was strict about ensuring that personal expenses were separated from company expenses and that the company funds were used only for company purposes. This showed a very strong sense of governance, thereby avoiding any improper use of company funds.

There is another aspect that I would like to point out, which may not have got the credit that it deserves. In my opinion, I consider this aspect extremely creditworthy and impressive. A fact, which many have overlooked, is that Premji's wealth would have been, in normal circumstances, passed on to the next generation. And this is no small amount. This can be judged by the fact that it is what has put Premji amongst the top 36 wealthiest people in the world. Now, with most of his wealth being given away, it is not being passed on to the next generation, instead, they are being asked to generate their own wealth. The family does own the financial interests in 7 per cent of the family holdings (which are left from Premji's shareholdings), which is a significant sum by itself, but which pales in comparison to what has been given away. So, what Premji has done is to create a strong base for the next generation to operate from, and provided for them adequately. But he has also ensured that the next generation has been challenged to create value, and consequently, their wealth. Given Premji's track record, it is a big responsibility, and his successors will have huge shoes to fill!

Readers may recall that a few years ago, there was a movement by the rich billionaires across the world—giving away their wealth as part of Bill and Melinda Gates and Warren Buffet's Giving Pledge (givingpledge.org). Whether the giving was as a commitment to the Giving Pledge or his own beliefs, one does not know. But his actions will have a deep impact on society.

Bill and Melinda Gates and Warren Buffet's Giving Pledge is a commitment by billionaires globally to give half or more of their wealth to philanthropic or charitable causes during their lifetime or in their wills. The donors can choose any field or cause to which they would like to contribute, to help make the world better. These fields could include poverty alleviation, refugee aid, disaster relief, global health, education, women and girls' empowerment, medical research, arts and culture, criminal justice reform or environmental sustainability. Premji is one of the signatories to this pledge, though his contribution to social causes had started much before. Premji was the first Indian to give away more than $2 billion to Giving Pledge in 2013. In recent years, more Indian billionaires have stepped up their philanthropic activities. Apart from the Nilekanis, Biocon founder Kiran Mazumdar-Shaw, Symphony Group's Romesh Wadhwani and realty tycoon P.N.C. Menon have pledged part of their wealth to the Gates-inspired Giving Pledge.[45]

Another belief which is held by some of the largest families having immense wealth is that one would effectively destroy the next generation if one transfers huge wealth to them. This has been seen in some cases globally, where US tycoons understood this and gave away a huge portion of their wealth for public welfare. Maybe this could be another reason why Premji did not transfer the wealth to the next generation and preferred to give it away.

VALUES AND ETHICS

Premji raised a very important point with the train ticket

---

[45]'History of the Pledge', Givingpledge.org, accessed 5 September 2019, https://givingpledge.org/About.aspx

incident, where the Wipro employee falsified his ticket claim, which I think offers a great learning opportunity for leaders. This is a topic which is highly debatable, and often leads to very charged and emotional discussions, whenever it is discussed. And I would like to take this opportunity to raise this here. Some readers may think that the instance may have been an overreaction and perhaps a warning to the employee would have sufficed. And that, maybe, it was an issue blown out of proportion.

My counterpoint is, was the amount really too small to have really mattered?

Premji was sincere to the extent of being almost stubborn-minded in pursuing his values without any compromises. He had his principles which he adhered to, without any pressures from any external sources requiring him to do so.

The bigger issue was not the quantum of the amount that was falsified for the false train ticket claim and that the employee had charged a first-class fare when he had actually travelled by second class. But the issue was, if an exception was made, then at what level would one draw the line? Or at what value would one decide that it was not acceptable? And who would decide the bar, beyond which the behaviour would be unacceptable?

If one were to take a philosophical stand, then, it has been pointed out by others that companies that allow small acts of integrity violations to take place within the firm are also those who commit major frauds outside the firm. Any leniency in allowing acts of corruption, howsoever small, would mean that the company culture allows deviations from the accepted behaviour. It could also mean that the company even considers these deviant activities as legitimate business activities. Such acts, for example, under a lenient or compliant government, may lead to crony capitalism, which has been plaguing India for many years in the past. This corruption leads to unproductive and wasteful usage of resources. These may serve the interests of an industrialist, but these acts cause great harm to the free markets, on which capitalism is based. In light of these, Premji's constant, non-negotiable war on corruption seemed like a breath of fresh air![46]

Let's assume, for example, in another company, a similar incident was an issue where ₹100 had been condoned. Then would the same behaviour, for, say, ₹500, also be condoned? Or for ₹50,000 by a senior executive? Or for ₹5,00,000 for a top-management team member? As one can see, this becomes a very slippery slope. And it becomes difficult to stop, once someone starts to go down this path.

Leaders often have to face dilemmas and uncertain environments where they are tested. These cases would test their resolve in holding on to what they consider valuable. The situations may be different and leaders could be tempted to assume that the situation is unique, unforeseen and exceptional. Hence, one would be justified in crossing the line and making an exception in the values which one may be following. The learning here is that an exception made once would lead to

---

[46]Varun Sood and Sundeep Khanna, 'Making of Azim Premji: The Philanthropist', *Livemint*, 24 June 2019, accessed 28 June 2019, https://www.livemint.com/companies/people/making-of-azim-premji-the-philanthropist-1561390035003.html

situations where one would cross the line multiple times in the future. And every time one could rationalize by stating that this was an exception under the prevailing circumstances and that there had been deviations in the past which were allowed.

This was also explained by Clayton Christensen, a professor at the Harvard Business School, in his article, 'How Will You Measure Your Life?'[47] Prof. Christensen states that the lesson that he had learnt is that it is easier to hold on to your principles 100 per cent of the time than it is to hold on to them 98 per cent of the time. He called this the marginal cost analysis, where if one considered making an exception just for one time, it does not seem to be high. And then, one gets pulled in, and one does not look at where the path is finally leading to, or the full cost that the 'just one time' decision entails. It is worth thinking over Christensen's statement, 'Justification for infidelity and dishonesty in all their manifestations lies in the marginal cost economics of 'just this once'. This means that all dishonesty or wrongdoing arises from our compromising once, thinking that a one-time exception to a rule would not cause any difference to our standards'.

If one considers Premji's actions in light of the above statements, then perhaps this would explain, to some extent, Premji's refusal to accept any compromise on integrity and dishonesty. By sending a clear message across the organization—that there were going to be no exceptions for any deviations in behaviour, and no compromises would be allowed in their values—Premji set a very clear deterrent for

---

[47]Clayton M. Christensen, 'How Will You Measure Your Life?', *Harvard Business Review*, pg. 46–51, July–August 2010

any such acts. And the message was clear, that there was going to be zero acceptance for any violation. This very clear message would permeate through the entire organization. And every time anyone was sacked, the message reaffirmed that there were no exceptions. This would ensure that the values were being enforced, without exceptions.

I have taken some liberty to elaborate on this point here, as this is one dimension that I find leaders grappling with today. Leaders have to lay down the rules and the exceptions, if any; what they are willing to overlook. And more importantly, what they are not willing to compromise on. Very often, and this comes from Christensen's findings, if we look at some of the organizations that are considered 'unethical', where the people have not been imprisoned for wrong acts, this would be because someone, somewhere in the organization, has thought that 'under normal circumstances, this act should not be done, but this one time, it is okay'. And this leads to the downfall of most organizations or the integrity of the people within. It is only when leaders in organizations stand up and state, unequivocally, that there will be no exceptions, and their principles are non-negotiable and not to be compromised, that we get organizations of integrity and values. The path is extremely tough. But the question is—do you have it in you to stand up and resist the temptation? The best leaders often do!

4
DEDICATION TO VALUES

ॐ

Azim Premji has built a large, well-respected business organization on a bedrock of integrity. The commitment to the 'Spirit of Wipro' (the values of the firm) is the soul of the company. I think he would be proud that he has been able to play by the rules and still succeed.[48]
—Rishad Premji

The Spirit of Wipro comprises four values:[49]

1. Be passionate about clients' successes
2. Be global and responsible

---

[48]Harichandan Arakali, 'Holding Wealth, the Azim Premji Way', *Forbes India*, 9 December 2016, accessed 30 June 2019, http://www.forbesindia.com/article/india-rich-list-2016/holding-wealth-the-azim-premji-way/45077/1

[49]'About Wipro', Wipro.com, accessed 30 June, 2019, https://www.wipro.com/about-us/

3. Treat each person with respect
4. Unyielding integrity in everything we do

Azim Premji, along with every person at Wipro, has been following these principles and using them to guide their behaviour and actions in everything that they do.

'The Spirit of Wipro' envisages all of Premji's business values in how to conduct business with integrity. For instance, an audit committee was set up by Wipro even though it was still not mandated by law, and giving bribes or favours to win a contract was a strict no-no. Premji also led some of the most pathbreaking people's initiatives, which have become a norm for most companies. Employee stock options, diversity and skill development are a few of these.

'Wipro always made heavy investments in training functions to develop people,' Soota said.[50] Wipro may have seen many changes in the nature of the firm, but Premji's values have remained constant, and these have been the benchmark on which the culture at Wipro has been defined. Suresh Senapaty, a Board member at Wipro Enterprises and former CFO, has said, 'As a leader, there are two things that stand out for me. The first is the values that he (Premji) lives by. He practises what he preaches and it has inspired the organization and me personally. Second, is the professionalism that he demonstrates. He creates an empowering environment and has allowed me unlimited opportunity to expand my horizons.'[51]

---

[50]Rukmini Rao, 'The Visionary', *Business Today*, 19 March 2019, accessed 1 June 2019, https://www.businesstoday.in/magazine/best-ceos-2019/the-visionary/story/318667.html
[51]Ibid.

LEARNINGS

The history of Wipro shows growth with a sense of integrity. Premji had identified a set of values that he deemed as valuable and then ensured that the firm also followed them. We find many examples of family-owned firms that have a strong influence of the promoter's style and values. This influence extends to every aspect of how the firm operates and behaves with all the other stakeholders (that is, everyone involved in or affected by the firm). In this case, Premji's values left a lasting influence on Wipro.

I remember interviewing one industrialist who was also known for acting with integrity in his group, and he had admitted, in a moment of candour, that his group had not been able to grow as fast as another of his peers. This was attributed to his insistence on remaining steadfast to their values and refusing to enter into certain industry sectors or choosing the business they accepted. So, wanting to work with integrity and adherence to one's values does have a steep price to pay, which can reflect in terms of lower growth and maybe fewer business opportunities. But every industrialist I have met had no regrets of following the path of integrity, in spite of the consequences. This was a cost that they were happy to pay. (I have not had the privilege of meeting Premji to confirm this, but I have no reservations in assuming, based on his actions till now, that this is the path he has taken, and he would undoubtedly agree to that!)

We talked in the previous chapter about leaders choosing not to compromise on their values, to any extent. And this is an important characteristic of great industrialists. They are clear on what they stand for, and are steadfast and not willing to step down from them. Their success is even sweeter since they know that they have achieved it on their terms, without any sacrifices.

The other effect they also have is the influence on the employees, who also get immersed in the same culture and start having the same beliefs. We have seen in many cases that the people working for a company become closely identified with the culture of the company they are working for.

5

WILLINGNESS TO EXPERIMENT AND LEARN

◖◗

When Azim Premji was handed over the responsibility of taking over the then fledgling, Western India Vegetable Products Ltd (Western India) in 1966, he had no idea how to run a business. He had been studying to be an engineer at Stanford University with the eventual idea of joining the World Bank to become a policymaker and help to develop the Third World. But as fate would determine otherwise, he was asked to run the family business, about which, he admitted, he had no clue.[52]

He, however, did not give up. He approached a professor at a leading management school in Mumbai (then Bombay) to ask for his recommendations for a list of textbooks. Premji

---

[52] Steve Hamm, *Bangalore Tiger, How Indian Tech Upstart Wipro Is Rewriting the Rules of Global Competition*, pg. 32, Tata McGraw-Hill Edition, India, 2007

had realized that the responsibilities of running a business full-time would leave him with no time for management education. Hence, he would have to learn on his own. He spent late nights and early mornings reading these textbooks and absorbing the learnings therein.[53]

Premji recalls his experience when he had first taken over at Wipro (then Western India). He admits that he learnt by accompanying his salespeople to the markets. He was going from shop to shop, trying to convince the shop owners to stock the vegetable oil that Western India manufactured at the time. This experience gave Premji an insight into the industry, and he realized how complex and demanding the sales job was. It also taught him a very valuable lesson that an organization was as good as its salespersons. It was then that he realized that the salespeople were the most important in the organization.[54]

He then used these lessons to instal modern management practices and processes in his company. Premji also listened to the advice of the old guard, the executives who had worked under his father, since they knew the business well. His company was suffering due to the lower priority it had got when it was run under his father. His father had been preoccupied in his efforts towards lobbying with the Central Government in New

---

[53] Steve Hamm, *Bangalore Tiger, How Indian Tech Upstart Wipro Is Rewriting the Rules of Global Competition*, pg. 32, Tata McGraw-Hill Edition, India, 2007

[54] Azim Premji, 'Don't Blame the Teacher: Azim Premji', *India Today*, 26 April 2018, accessed 30 June 2019, https://www.indiatoday.in/magazine/guest-column/story/20180507-azim-premji-column-on-indian-education-system-teachers-1221665-2018-04-26

Delhi, on various issues such as deregulating the foodgrains industry and helping to make policies, or serving on multiple industry Boards.[55] This was typical of most industry leaders at the time, since fortunes could be made or lost based on the vagaries of the industrial policy that influenced every step that a business could take. This left very little time to devote to the business, hence the business suffered and languished and often took a back seat.

He is known to be interested in learning. His people define him as being in a constant learning mode. Premji was not knowledgeable about the IT business but he decided to learn from the people whom he hired to run and build the IT business. He was also a constant participant in the interviews for all recruits, as this practice helped him to build new talent and additionally helped him to understand the IT business.[56]

Premji is willing to experiment and is not afraid to take tough decisions if necessary. A case in point is his appointment of co-CEOs in 2008. He felt that two executives' abilities would complement each other. This was an unprecedented move, and perhaps unusual. But this did not work out, and the company was losing ground to other new and nimbler competitors. Azim Premji took a tough call to end this structure in 2011,

---

[55] Steve Hamm, *Bangalore Tiger, How Indian Tech Upstart Wipro is Rewriting the Rules of Global Competition*, pg. 32, Tata McGraw-Hill, India, 2007

[56] Varun Sood and Sundeep Khanna, 'Making of Azim Premji: The Philanthropist', *Livemint*, 24 June 2019, accessed 28 June 2019, https://www.livemint.com/companies/people/making-of-azim-premji-the-philanthropist-1561390035003.html

since it was not working. He reverted to a single CEO model and brought in a new person for the role.[57]

LEARNINGS

The above stories show Azim Premji's willingness to learn and assimilate. He also demonstrated the ability to recognize what he did not know and he made efforts to make up for this lack of knowledge. He also sought to learn from experts, with the understanding that he did not know everything, and did not just reject old thoughts and practices for the new.

He knew that he had to bring in the newer processes, especially when he had taken over. But this did not mean that the old was completely redundant. His humility to learn from the old executives shows that he did not have the arrogance of being the owner of the company. He respected the executives who had been running the businesses earlier and learnt from their experience. But at the same time, he was realistic enough to understand that he needed to fill the gap in his knowledge. Formal management education was not possible at the time, so he took it upon himself to find out where he could learn things, and had the discipline to learn by himself.

The key learning here is that one needs to, oftentimes, take a realistic assessment of one's capabilities, and realize that one is not perfect. This realization will only come when

---

[57]Harichandan Arakali, 'Holding Wealth, the Azim Premji Way', *Forbes India*, 9 December 2016, accessed 30 June 2019, http://www.forbesindia.com/article/india-rich-list-2016/holding-wealth-the-azim-premji-way/45077/1

one is humble enough. But we find that leaders mostly live under the illusion of being superhuman, and capable enough to handle any subject. This may have been true in earlier times when basic common sense was sufficient to survive, but in today's times of superspecialization and the need for a high level of technical knowledge in certain industries, it may cause challenges. (On a different note, I don't disregard the need for common sense, which I think is needed also, for success!)

The key learning highlighted in this chapter is for one to experiment and try out new things. As we will see in a later chapter, there is an example of transition from the business that Wipro was in, moving from vegetable oils to software coding to R&D and consulting. This shows that Premji was not stubbornly sticking to the tried and tested business which was profitable but dared to take risks by experimenting and venturing into newer areas. These experiments helped shape the success that Wipro is today. This comes from creating an environment of trust and encouraging experiments, and rewarding people for trying. This would also mean that failures would not be penalized or treated as career suicides for the individuals concerned, who tried and may have failed.

Hence, the strong desire to learn, to accept others more knowledgeable than yourself, and encouraging an environment to experiment and learn, is critical for managerial success. All are attributes that Azim Premji displayed.

6
WHAT GETS MEASURED GETS DONE

॰ॐ

Use modern tools to monitor performance and to get operational excellence.

Azim Premji had taken over his father's company under rather trying circumstances. He inherited a system which was based on traditional methods of management which he tried to change.

In the initial years, one of the first things that Premji did was to work on setting up a corporate culture and a management style. This was the foundation on which the edifice which was to become the current-day Wipro would be built. And this move laid the seeds for the first steps towards building the organization. If one had to elaborate on Premji's contribution which turned around the family firm, then I would guess that top on the list would have been the use of data for measurement and analysis that he had introduced. This was in total contrast to the way the business was done earlier during his father's time, where decision-making was based on traditions and instincts.[58]

To mention an example, the family firm was purchasing groundnuts from farmers at wholesale prices. These were dried in the open in the factory premises before being processed to produce vegetable oil. This was done in their factory at Amalner in Maharashtra.[59] These groundnuts were bought by the buyer on behalf of Western India. The buyer used a traditional way of determining the price for the purchase of the crop. He would take a few seeds in his hand, bite them and then estimate the oil content based on the taste! This system was the first one to be changed. Premji replaced this procedure by a simpler but more accurate process-based method. The new process involved getting samples from the farmers, drying the nuts and then weighing these to calculate the oil content. The prices would then be determined on this basis. This was one of the many steps that Azim Premji took to replace what was earlier a subjective, tradition-based 'art' into a technology-based business process.[60] This soon became one of the core competencies of the company and helped to make the company profitable.

However, the story does not stop here. The buyers soon felt redundant since their expertise was no longer required.

---

[58] Steve Hamm, *Bangalore Tiger, How Indian Tech Upstart Wipro is Rewriting the Rules of Global Competition*, pg. 32, Tata McGraw-Hill, India, 2007

[59] Pankaj Mishra, 'Hello, Azim Seth!', Factordaily.com, blog, 22 July 2016, accessed 29 June 2019, https://factordaily.com/hello-azim-seth/

[60] Steve Hamm, *Bangalore Tiger, How Indian Tech Upstart Wipro is Rewriting the Rules of Global Competition*, pg. 34, Tata McGraw-Hill, India, 2007

Premji quickly reconfigured their responsibilities and put them in charge of managing the business. They were trained to use data to monitor the retailers' sales, understand the demand and supply conditions and use this information for making more profitable pricing decisions. He took this a step further with his holding Monday morning staff meetings so that he could monitor and improve performance. This practice is something that Wipro does even today. What is interesting to note is that this practice had its genesis at a time when conference calling or direct dialling was not available, and one had to use operator assistance to call anyone outside the city! Premji had set up a process where his managers used the operator-assisted calls to call in, and report to him. He had given his managers the freedom to operate in their markets but they were held accountable for preset performance targets.[61]

In an article on Premji's ability to manage different verticals in Wipro's conglomerate structure, Soota had explained, 'He knew the factors that could lead to success in each one of those, and he measured people on those factors. He knew what was critical to each business.'[62]

Even during the software development days, Wipro used technology much ahead of its peers. It had used technology to develop dashboards on which Wipro managers kept track of the various teams working on the various 2000-odd projects

---

[61] Steve Hamm, *Bangalore Tiger, How Indian Tech Upstart Wipro is Rewriting the Rules of Global Competition*, pg. 34, Tata McGraw-Hill, India, 2007

[62] Rukmini Rao, 'The Visionary', Business Today, 10 March 2019, accessed 9 July 2019, https://www.businesstoday.in/magazine/best-ceos-2019/the-visionary/story/318667.html

that Wipro had going on, at any given point of time. It also maintained a digital folder of each of its employees, including their skills, projects done and the current projects they were engaged in. This enables their managers to search and select various team members needed for various newer projects. All the offices globally were connected by voice over internet protocol (VOIP) so that every Wipro employee was connected. These seem like everyday tools today, but at that time, these were state-of-the-art, cutting edge technologies. And Wipro used these effectively to communicate with its people all over the world across different geographical and time zones.[63]

LEARNING

Many would have guessed the use of technology in Premji's efforts to make his management more efficient. Although that is a partially correct answer, if one were to look at a much bigger picture, then one would realize that the biggest point to be appreciated here is the fact that Premji did not hesitate to change the current practices in favour of something more precise and modern.

Managers often are faced with situations where they find that old traditional processes and methods are being used. These could be systems, processes and methods that have been prevalent, maybe for a very long time, and have become a part of the culture of the company. Or maybe it is 'how

---

[63]Steve Hamm, *Bangalore Tiger, How Indian Tech Upstart Wipro is Rewriting the Rules of Global Competition*, pg. 26, Tata McGraw-Hill, India, 2007

things are done here', or the industry practice, which no one questions, and everyone accepts.

There could be situations where no one even knows who started certain practices, and why they are still being carried on. And in the absence of any motivation to change, one still finds these systems in place. The newcomer company, in a competitive environment, has the advantage of not being burdened by legacy and can question why such practices have to be followed. Perhaps even suggest alternatives if they have the power to effect such change. But the common thread with leaders, who are successful and can effect change, is that they have not accepted the status quo. They have found newer, better and more efficient ways to do things that were being done. Or even question if something needed to be done at all. Do we need to carry on doing the things that we have been doing? The leaders know that change comes in only when we have the courage to ask why we are doing what we are doing, and the conviction and dedication to stop doing the things that do not make sense. Of course, one would need to realize that the biggest resistance to change would come from those who are benefitting from keeping things as they are. For example, in Premji's case, probably from the buyers, whose livelihoods would have been threatened, since a new system would make them redundant. So, retraining them for a newer role was a wise move, since this one step converted the possible resistance to cooperation.

Another challenge that Premji faced and resolved was the fact that he replaced systems based on subjective methods by more scientific ones. There is a saying: 'What gets measured gets done'. Premji's drive to put in more measurement systems helped him understand what was happening in the business and take corrective action wherever needed, at the right time.

A point to be observed is how Premji had used technology to cut costs and improve productivity and increase efficiencies. The business environment is about reducing costs since one does not always have the luxury of raising prices all the time. This is especially true in today's competitive markets where the profits are getting constantly reduced due to increased competition. This is also leading to reduced prices as companies are forced to cut costs just to stay competitive. Amidst this situation, it makes sense to use technology to monitor and reduce wastage or increase productivity. The key assumption is that the cost of the technology should not be so high, that one can never recover the costs or ever be profitable! In this respect, Premji's initiatives helped make the company more efficient.

7

LEAD BY EXAMPLE: BE A ROLE MODEL TO EMULATE THE BEHAVIOUR THAT YOU WANT OTHERS TO FOLLOW

I think Wipro is his life. He loves it and cares for it as if it were his child. I think, as he has gotten older, he is very energized by the fact that the success of Wipro could have a great impact on his philanthropic work. He feels deeply about how privileged and lucky he has been and is very focused on doing all he can to give back (to society).[64]

—Rishad Premji

---

[64]Harichandan Arakali, 'Holding Wealth, the Azim Premji Way', *Forbes India*, 9 December 2016, accessed 30 June 2019, http://www.forbesindia.com/article/india-rich-list-2016/holding-wealth-the-azim-premji-way/45077/1

Azim Premji had always been dedicated to working hard. His elder son Rishad has early memories of his father spending a lot of time working at home on his desk, going through 'tonnes of files filled with notes and documents'.[65]

Rishad continues by saying, 'He still "comes to the office" is a very mild way of putting it. He may still be among the hardest-working people at Wipro. I have not seen anyone sustain the kind of work ethic and drive that he has, over such a long time. Perhaps my grandmother has been an influence; she ran her charitable hospital with the same energy, way past the age when most people retire.'[66]

Premji had explained once that what inspired him was the ambition to do better than what they were doing and to grow much faster than what they had been doing historically.[67]

Premji always went well-prepared for his meetings. His former CFO, Suresh Senapaty, recalls one instance—he was staying at Premji's house when, at 10 p.m., Premji handed over a thick box file of papers to him, which he had been studying for a meeting the next day. He asked Senapaty to return it to

---

[65]Harichandan Arakali, 'Holding Wealth, the Azim Premji Way', *Forbes India*, 9 December 2016, accessed 30 June 2019, http://www.forbesindia.com/article/india-rich-list-2016/holding-wealth-the-azim-premji-way/45077/1

[66]Ibid.

[67]Masoom Gupta, 'I Have Worked Very Hard and Neglected My Family: Azim Premji', *The Economic Times*, 17 February 2017, accessed 30 June 2019, https://economictimes.indiatimes.com/magazines/panache/i-have-worked-very-hard-and-neglected-my-family-azim-premji/articleshow/57198112.cms

him at 5 a.m. the next day, since he wanted to study it once more before their meeting. So, Azim Premji was going to go through the papers once again that early in the morning!

Premji was an early riser, would be up before sunrise and not sleep before midnight on most days. Additionally, he was also very respectful of all his people. He would not ask his team to do anything that he would not do himself. He was also described as a keen listener, asking deep insightful questions. He was known never to have directed or instructed his team, a result of his respect for his people.[68]

Another instance which is mentioned in detail later on in this book is his attention to detail, especially when hiring people. He worked on interviewing people to hire the right person, and even called each of the references given by the candidate personally, in the case of hiring people at the higher level.

In 2018, while interacting with school and college students during the Wipro Earthian awards ceremony, Premji was asked about his goal in life. He answered, 'To be successful in what I do and to the best of what I can do.'[69] It isn't surprising that this drives him even at the age of seventy-three.

Premji was always a role model for his people. His conduct and personal behaviour was not only a model but also an

---

[68]Suresh Senapaty, 'Opinion: Azim Premji, the Embodiment of Simple Living and High Thinking', *Livemint*, 9 April 2019, accessed 30 June 2019, https://www.livemint.com/opinion/columns/opinion-azim-premji-the-embodiment-of-simple-living-and-high-thinking-1554499738628.html

[69]Rukmini Rao, 'The Visionary', *Business Today*, 19 March 2019, accessed 1 June 2019, https://www.businesstoday.in/magazine/best-ceos-2019/the-visionary/story/318667.html

inspiration for others to emulate.

He was willing to work hard for long hours under trying conditions and expected his people to do the same. His normal workday is more than ten hours long and he is often seen working on weekends.

Another anecdote is from the early years of Western India when they were operating the factory at Amalner, about an eight-hour drive from Mumbai. (The factory is supposed to still be in operation today, manufacturing Santoor soap, one of the top-selling soap brands in its category in India.) The temperatures during summer used to touch 44–45°C and the company could not afford air conditioning during the time. The net result was that the production dipped during the summer months. Premji was aware of this and refused to accept this as a benchmark. He decided to do something about this and moved into the town one summer. He stayed there for three months. After this time, the summer production never dipped again.[70]

Learnings

Azim Premji is motivated and driven by his passion to work hard. This is even though he does not need to, as his existing wealth is more than enough to accomplish all his desires! But the discipline and the dedication that he brings to the table speaks volumes about his drive to achieve much more than just financial gains. It is almost as if he is driven by a mission

---

[70]Steve Hamm, *Bangalore Tiger, How Indian Tech Upstart Wipro is Rewriting the Rules of Global Competition*, pg. 34, Tata McGraw-Hill, India, 2007

to work hard so that he can contribute more to philanthropy! He is also driven by a very strong sense of purpose. His benchmark for comparison is only himself, which he seeks to improve. This is a very positive way of working, since it is not a competitive situation, except maybe with himself. So it is a healthy situation where one is seeking to improve oneself.

The other aspect is that Azim Premji's habit of working hard serves as an example for others in the firm to emulate. And this proves to be a fine example of leading by setting an example. The others cannot complain if the topmost person is putting in such dedication and devotion!

His willingness to dive into an issue and get his feet wet is a trait that very few industrialists possess. The successful ones have gone into the field and worked on the ground level realities, and found solutions at that level. These solutions would probably be more acceptable and practically relevant. He did not shoot orders from his executive corporate office. He had a very good understanding of his business, which most successful leaders have. His recognition of the salesman being the most important person in the company is a rare insight which not many have understood, as the salesman is responsible for the actual sale and for bringing the cash into the company. All other functional areas are not necessarily generating revenues but are incurring costs. Hence, the realization of the importance of the sales area, as a vital component of the company from a very early time, is interesting and shows the keen insights which came from logical reasoning, even though Premji did not have any experience of business or any business management education!

8
DIVERSIFY AND SEIZE OPPORTUNITIES

☙

Azim Premji had grabbed every opportunity that he had been presented with. He took over the steering wheel at Wipro after the death of his father in 1966. This was against the Board members' wishes who wanted more experienced management to take over. He, however, took over, regardless of their wishes, and soon turned the company around using modern technology-based and data-driven decisions. Once the company was profitable, Premji realized that he had to do more.

He had also realized that he had to broaden his business beyond cooking oil. He had seen opportunities and he wanted to capture them. He also had seen the examples of the Western companies in the 1970s that had formed conglomerates by buying over businesses in unrelated areas and had gone global. The idea behind this action was to ensure that the earnings are constant; as the assumption would be that the different industries would have different cycles of profitability. And this would help; as a down-cycle in one industry could be offset by an uptick in the other industry; thus the company would make at least a steady minimum level of profits. This was an effective strategy followed by the major US corporates, and Premji decided to follow suit for Wipro. He moved into soaps and beauty products.[71]

Premji recalls that Wipro was then into the commodity cooking oil sector and used to sell their products in the wholesale markets. They decided to grow their business by moving into the retail business, set up a distribution business and launch their own brand. Investing in a manufacturing plant was their first step into soap manufacturing. They faced several difficulties initially, including a failed launch of their first product. They relaunched their Santoor brand, which became successful and Wipro moved into the toiletries business, and never looked back.[72]

He also moved into manufacturing hydraulic components for construction equipment, making Western India Vegetable Products into a small conglomerate with revenues of about $30 million. At this time, in 1977, Premji changed the name of the company to Wipro Products Ltd.[73]

---

[71]Varun Sood and Sundeep Khanna, 'Making of Azim Premji: The Philanthropist', *Livemint*, 24 June 2019, accessed 28 June 2019, https://www.livemint.com/companies/people/making-of-azim-premji-the-philanthropist-1561390035003.html

[72]Anil Dharkar, 'Bhaskar Interview: Joh Sampann Hai, Unhe Garibo Ke Behtar Jeevan Ke Liye Kuch Na Kuch Karna Chahiye: Azim Premji', *Dainik Bhaskar*, 29 July 2019, accessed 25 August 2019, https://www.bhaskar.com/national/news/wipro-chairman-azim-premji-retires-01605177.html

[73]Varun Sood and Sundeep Khanna, 'Making of Azim Premji: The

SECOND COMING

The second opportunity came in 1979, when the Government of India changed policies and consequently compelled the exodus of many multinational global companies from India, including IBM and Coca-Cola. This led to a huge demand for computer hardware and Premji stepped up with products manufactured by Wipro to fill the gap. Wipro started to assemble computers and other electronic products. This was helped by the fact, that the imports into India were banned or had very high-duty tariffs, thus making imports very expensive. His factories were set up in Bengaluru, where the weather conditions were favourable for electronics assembly.[74] This helped Wipro become a significantly large manufacturer of technology hardware.

Premji changed the name to Wipro in 1977.[75] He had set up multiple international partnerships successfully, which helped it to manufacture computer hardware in India to sell in the domestic markets. By the end of 1982, Wipro became a manufacturer and marketer of microprocessor-based computer systems, under a technology-sharing agreement with US-based Sentinel Computers Ltd.[76] And

---

Philanthropist', *Livemint*, 24 June 2019, accessed 28 June 2019, https://www.livemint.com/companies/people/making-of-azim-premji-the-philanthropist-1561390035003.html

[74]Yaroslav Trofimov, 'How a Muslim Billionaire Thrives in Hindu India', *The Wall Street Journal*, 11 September 2007, accessed 29 June 2019, https://www.wsj.com/articles/SB118947228823323260

[75]Anthony G. Craine, 'Azim Premji', *Encyclopaedia Britannica*, accessed 29 June 2019, https://www.britannica.com/biography/Azim-Premji

[76]Harish Puppala and Rakesh Sharma, 'Digging Deeper—Azim Premji:

in 1983, Wipro spun the Information Technology Division into a wholly-owned subsidiary.[77] In 1989, Wipro had a joint venture with GE for the manufacture, sales and service of diagnostic and imaging products under the name of Wipro GE Medical Systems, which became a subsidiary of Wipro, in the year 1990.[78]

In 1990, Wipro entered the IT services arena. Premji moved into hardware manufacturing with foreign collaborations. This was the time when Wipro Systems was started. This became the first product company in India to launch a 16-bit multitasking computer. Then, in 1999, Wipro became the only Indian Personal Computer (PC) maker to obtain a National Software Testing Laboratory Certification.[79]

In 1999–2000, Wipro was a leading software exporter, ahead of Infosys, with software exports of ₹10.5 billion, compared with Infosys' ₹8.52 billion.[80]

The End of an Era', Moneycontrol.com, accessed 30 June, 2019, https://www.moneycontrol.com/news/podcast/digging-deeper-azim-premji-the-end-of-an-era-4090341.html; Wipro.com, accessed 5 September 2019, https://www.wipro.com/en-IN/about-us/

[77]Varun Sood and Sundeep Khanna, 'Making of Azim Premji: The Philanthropist', Livemint, 24 June 2019, accessed 28 June 2019, https://www.livemint.com/companies/people/making-of-azim-premji-the-philanthropist-1561390035003.html

[78]Harish Puppala and Rakesh Sharma, 'Digging Deeper—Azim Premji: The End of an Era', Moneycontrol.com, accessed 30 June 2019, https://www.moneycontrol.com/news/podcast/digging-deeper-azim-premji-the-end-of-an-era-4090341.html

[79]Ibid.

[80]Rukmini Rao, 'The Visionary', Business Today, 19 March 2019, accessed 1 June 2019, https://www.businesstoday.in/magazine/best-ceos-2019/the-visionary/story/318667.html

Diversify and Seize Opportunities

Addressing Stanford business graduates in 2006, Premji spoke about the IT services bet. 'It's easier to make money in services with lower risks than it is in products,' Premji said, answering the question whether India would ever become a product business powerhouse.

At this time, Premji became known for hiring the best people and providing them with very high quality training. India then had a very large pool of well-educated software developers, whose labour costs were much lower than the costs of the American developers. Wipro used this fact to their advantage, and built up their custom software export business, exporting software predominantly to the US. Subsequently, the software business emerged as their largest business, turning Wipro, alongside Tata Consultancy Services (TCS) and Infosys, as one of the leading and most respected IT services firms in India.[81]

The steps that Premji took—moving away from the stable margins of the vegetable oil business, to entering unchartered waters of the IT business—required a lot of courage and vision. Nevertheless, as history would show, Premji had this in spades as he led his company over multiple changes.

This growth path did not last long, as, in the 1990s, the government changed. They came up with a new policy that was in tune with the growing global trend of the rise of capitalism. This was led by the Eastern European nations,

---

[81] Harish Puppala, Rakesh Sharma, 'Digging Deeper—Azim Premji: The End of an Era', Moneycontrol.com, accessed 30 June 2019, https://www.moneycontrol.com/news/podcast/digging-deeper-azim-premji-the-end-of-an-era-4090341.html

which had converted to capitalism to kick-start growth in their respective economies. The import restrictions, under which Wipro had till then thrived, were eased.

This was also the time, just before the turn of the century, where the Y2K bug fear had gripped the companies globally. This was the fear that the software code that was running most companies' systems may have defined the years as a two-digit field instead of a four-digit field. For example, 1999 is defined as '99'. This would mean that at the turn of the century, the systems would go from 1999 to 1900 instead of 2000. This would be because the computer systems may not be able to recognize the turn of the century and hence it was feared that all the systems would crash and their activities would be affected. To overcome this issue, all the organizations had to go through their code, rewriting code where needed, to ensure that the IT infrastructure did not fail. This caused a huge surge in the businesses of software companies, including that of Wipro.

The software services path was a new one being explored by Wipro. It used the quality accreditations route to differentiate itself from its competitors. It got certified under different quality standards to demonstrate its commitment and capabilities. It became the first company to explore offshore IT services in the 1990s. In 1999, it became the first and only Indian computer manufacturer to get certified as Y2K-compliant by the US-based National Software Testing Laboratory.[82] Wipro was also one of the first software

---

[82]Harish Puppala and Rakesh Sharma, 'Digging Deeper—Azim Premji: The End of an Era', Moneycontrol.com, accessed 30 June 2019, https://

Diversify and Seize Opportunities 57

companies to get SEI Level 5 certification. These may have played an important role in Wipro, which, in 2004, registered revenue of a billion dollars for the first time.

THE THIRD ACT

But soon the environment changed and the customers were no longer needing Wipro's goods and services, as they could buy the best available products from the global markets. According to a Wipro executive, this may have caused an existential challenge for Wipro, as it did for many of Wipro's peers who did not survive this drastic change.[83]

Premji grabbed this opportunity and went to his customers, the foreign companies with whom Wipro had done business as a manufacturer and as a software developer. These were established and reputed companies such as GE and Sun Microsystems. Premji realized that he had low cost but high quality engineers in Wipro. He asked his customers, 'Why don't you contract your design, research and testing as an outsourced service to Wipro (instead of doing it yourselves)?'

Wipro's game plan worked. It soon found out that its outsourcing business grew exponentially, spanning the entire range, from call centres to designing mobile phones for leading international players. It also began managing the computer

---

www.moneycontrol.com/news/podcast/digging-deeper-azim-premji-the-end-of-an-era-4090341.html

[83]Yaroslav Trofimov, 'How a Muslim Billionaire Thrives in Hindu India', *The Wall Street Journal*, 11 September 2007, accessed 29 June 2019, https://www.wsj.com/articles/SB118947228823323260

systems of European utilities and carrying out full-service business consulting.[84]

LEARNINGS

Wipro, under Premji, has shown remarkable resilience in understanding the new changes in the environment. It has worked to change itself and to modify and equip itself to face the newer challenges of the markets, thus ensuring that it can offer newer services to customers; services that they now need. This is an extremely important quality that leaders should have; to explore the new, while continuing to exploit the old businesses.

The move into soap manufacturing offers an interesting learning for managers. Usually one finds limited growth in the area that one is primarily operating in. One has the option to remain stagnant and satisfied by the existing growth, or look at additional areas of growth. Wipro, under Premji, moved from the commodity segment to the retail segment with a branded soap. This was not an easy step, as they had to steer away from their comfort zone and do things that could be quite difficult and expensive. Like setting up a distribution channel, or investing in a plant and machinery to manufacture soap. This takes a long-term commitment, which Premji was ready to make.

So, there were three things happening here at this stage,

---

[84]Yaroslav Trofimov, 'How a Muslim Billionaire Thrives in Hindu India', *The Wall Street Journal*, 11 September 2007, accessed 29 June 2019, https://www.wsj.com/articles/SB118947228823323260

that offer rich learnings:

1. Related diversification: Moving into soaps was a smart move, as it was a diversification into a related area adjoining their industry, that is, of vegetable oils. This would offer an easier path as compared to diversification into an unrelated area.
2. From commodity to branded products: Premji moved from a commodity business to branded retail. It was a known fact that the margins were higher in the branded segment, so this offered an attractive segment to move into. (Of course, this step also depended on the capability of the firm to set up a branded product, the distribution channels, and investments in advertising and marketing.) Additionally, there are also higher costs for setting up this entire infrastructure for the brand to be successful, but if one is lucky and works on it, they may make profits that would take care of these higher costs.

    We have seen similar examples where original bulk manufacturers have moved into making products under their own brands which offered a potentially more profitable segment for managers to consider. This is the path that some firms follow, from commodities to branded products, using services and experiences, to differentiate their brands in the pursuit of higher profits.
3. Not worrying about sunk costs when evaluating new businesses: Let us first understand the concept of sunk costs. Sunk costs are those costs that have been incurred and cannot be recovered. Usually managers keep these costs in mind while considering future investments. So,

for example, if a new product has to be launched, but will need fresh investments, and make the previously made capital expenditures on the plant and machinery for the existing older product redundant, then there will be resistance from the manager of the older product, wanting to keep the older product alive. The main argument that would be given is that the organizational investments would go waste. This thought could force them to continue at a maybe marginal profit or a breakeven level. Hence, companies that preferred to keep the existing product lines alive to protect their investments would divert resources away from new projects. This is why new products are not being launched in such organizations. This is something that managers should be sensitive to and should understand, while making decisions. Of course, it worked well for Wipro. The company would not have been a successful toiletry products brand, had it exited at that time! The fact that the investment had already been made placed pressure on the company to use it and hence stay in the business, instead of quitting. These pressures were oftentimes the reasons why companies chose to stay in industries which were not as profitable.

Many may wonder about the entry of Wipro into the IT sector from soaps and vegetable oils. In an interview given by Premji, he explained that at the time there was no separate field known as IT. Premji's computer science background helped, as everything was termed to be included under the subject of computer science at that time. It was only later on that IT was carved out to create a separate identity for itself. Premji related a story of how F.C. Kohli, the industrialist, was asked to head TCS as its first chief. When informed about this, Kohli had reportedly said to J.R.D. Tata that he did not know anything about IT. Tata is said to have retorted that no one knew anything about computers, and he pointed out that Kohli at least had a degree in electrical engineering![85]

The evolution of Wipro from a hardware manufacturer to a software coding services provider to a solutions and R&D outsourced supplier has ensured its relevance over the years where other competitors in similar markets faced difficulties to manage, to sustain, and were forced to exit.

What changes do you bring to a company?

Another tool that leaders can use is the concept of having a fresh look or looking at the current business with a fresh set of eyes. Simply put, in other words, if you were hired as a fresh employee in the company, what changes would you make?

The importance of this approach cannot be overstated. In fact, most existing companies that find themselves unable to compete, fall into this trap, since they are beaten by newer competitors who do not have to follow tradition, or worry about using legacy assets or systems, and hence are able to design companies to be more competitive and responsive.

The classic example of Intel and Andy Grove would be

---

[85]Anil Dharkar, 'Bhaskar Interview: Joh Sampann Hai, Unhe Garibo Ke Behtar JeevanK Liye Kuch Na Kuch Karna Chahiye: Azim Premji', *Dainik Bhaskar*, 29 July 2019, accessed 25 August 2019, https://www.bhaskar.com/national/news/wipro-chairman-azim-premji-retires-01605177.html

relevant here.[86] Grove was the president and Gordon Moore was the CEO of US-based Intel, a microprocessor company. The company made memory semiconductors (also called chips), which went into the computers. But Intel was getting beaten by the Japanese, who were able to produce in much higher volumes and beat Intel at costs. The Japanese had successfully converted the memory chip into a commodity and was beating Intel. Intel refused to believe that they were beaten and continued to invest in a losing market. At the time, in 1985, Grove asked Gordon, 'If we got kicked out and the Board brought in a new CEO, what do you think he would do?'

Gordon answered without hesitation, 'He would get us out of memories.' (Memory chips)

Andy stared at Gordon, and answered with what has now become a classic statement, 'Why shouldn't you and I walk out the door, come back, and do it ourselves?'

And the rest is history. What one needs to find, is the will to let go, even if painful, to do the right thing.

If we look at Premji's journey at Wipro, we find similar cases of radical decisions made. In a later chapter on diversification, we see that Premji faced almost a crisis at Wipro, at least twice. And he had to decide on changing the path that Wipro was on. This seemed like such a big risk at the time, but that is what eventually played a very important role in saving the company.

---

[86]Richard Tedlow, 'Fortune Classic: The Education of Andy Grove', *Fortune*, 21 March 2016, accessed 9 July 2019, https://fortune.com/2016/03/21/andy-grove-fortune-classic/

9

TRAIN AND MENTOR YOUR PEOPLE WELL

In a talk to the graduating class of Indian School of Business (ISB), Hyderabad, Premji related his story of the mid-1970s, when Wipro was a small company manufacturing vegetable oils, and had just started diversifying into making soap.

He stated that he remembered the early days of Wipro. At the time, it was just a small manufacturer of vegetable oils, which had just begun its diversification into soap manufacturing. He was aware that he needed a good team if his company had to grow and that having the right people would probably work out the issues of strategy and other important issues. Keeping this in mind, he decided to recruit the best people from the best places, and this thought led him to the Indian Institute of Management, Ahmedabad (IIMA).

He set out to recruit people from IIMA when he was still in his early twenties. Premji thought that it may have seemed presumptuous on his part, as he was just in his early twenties, owning a small unknown company. Premji realized that most of the business school graduates would want to work for his blue-chip competitors—companies like Hindustan Lever, which was the leader in their product category at the time and about a hundred times the size of Premji's company! Premji further recalled that they were not taken very seriously at the time, and he was not even allowed to have a dialogue with the students.

That year, he had to return home empty-handed. But Premji was not discouraged, and he continued to work on this task. He continued to represent Wipro in a frank and straightforward manner, trying, at many reputed institutions, to attract the recent graduates, but it was three years of painstaking efforts before this showed any results. Premji achieved success with a couple of recruits before the steady stream started, and by the 1980s, Wipro started being invited to top business school campuses for recruitment.

Premji further stated that the business school graduates, who joined Wipro, clearly understood Wipro and what it stood for before they joined. Premji credits the long-tenured careers that people have in Wipro, after they have joined, to this fact. And most of these people play a significant role in influencing the future of Wipro.

> The thing about being comfortable with who and what you are, and presenting that with candour, has always stood us in good stead. In fact, now our clients tell us that this is one of the big advantages that they find in

dealing with us, vis-à-vis our competitors.

—Azim Premji's address to ISB students[87]

The 1980s shaped the future of Wipro. As mentioned earlier, Premji pursued Ashok Soota to head the IT division and to grow its IT business. (The subsidiary that handled the IT business was demerged from the non-IT business subsequently.) Soota was sceptical initially, but as already mentioned, he agreed to take up Premji's offer to head Wipro's products business. The process of hiring and the degree of personal interest that Premji had was unique for a person of his stature. Apart from making it a new learning phase for Soota, it was also a new phase of growth for the company. As mentioned earlier, in the case of hiring Soota, we had seen how detailed Premji was. This was done just to ensure that the right person was being hired. Hence, the biggest strengths were the people that Premji had handpicked.[88]

(Soota went on to become a co-founder in Mindtree and is currently the chairman of Happiest Mind, an IT services company. Soota also stated that he had dedicated his book, *Entrepreneurship Simplified: From Idea to IPO* to Premji, one of the three people from whom he learnt the most.)[89]

---

[87] Arun Srivastava, 'In Praise of the Ordinary', Speakingtree.in, 4 May 2014, accessed 9 July 2019, https://www.speakingtree.in/blog/in-praise-of-the-ordinary,

[88] Raghu Krishnan, 'Azim Premji's Strength Is the People He Picks: Ashok Soota', *The Economic Times*, 7 June 2019, accessed 30 June 2019, https://economictimes.indiatimes.com/tech/ites/azim-premjis-strength-is-the-people-he-picks-ashok-soota/articleshow/69684052.cms

[89] Rukmini Rao, 'The Visionary', *Business Today*, 19 March 2019, accessed

Even if we consider the case of Premji's philanthropic foundations, these have been run by hand-picked professionals, Anurag Behar and Dileep Ranjekar.

It was not just the hand-picking but also the fact that Premji empowered his people. He took detailed notes to understand the issues at hand. He also used to give a lot of freedom to the people who reported to him. He was not necessarily one who delegated everything; he was also hands-on. He was very detail-oriented, used to ask a lot of questions, and added a lot of value whenever he participated in the decision-making process. But if any of his people took a decision, Premji would honour it and not overrule it and let the executives take responsibility and power.[90]

In an interview with Subroto Bagchi, founder of Mindtree, who worked under Premji, Bagchi stated that the greatness of Premji was his ability to surround himself with people who, in their areas, were more competent than he was. He was also happy to get some pushback from them as the professionals questioned his ideas and may not have always agreed with his suggestions.[91]

---

1 June 2019, https://www.businesstoday.in/magazine/best-ceos-2019/the-visionary/story/318667.html

[90] Raghu Krishnan, 'Azim Premji's Strength Is the People He Picks: Ashok Soota', *The Economic Times*, 7 June 2019, accessed 30 June 2019, https://economictimes.indiatimes.com/tech/ites/azim-premjis-strength-is-the-people-he-picks-ashok-soota/articleshow/69684052.cms

[91] Subroto Bagchi, 'Patriotic Businessman: Ex-colleague Subroto Bagchi on Azim Premji', The Quint, 13 June 2019, accessed 30 June 2019, https://www.thequint.com/videos/news-videos/subroto-bagchi-on-azim-premji-wipro-chairperson

Premji's integrity was clear, and in black and white. He did not believe in playing around since he realized that, otherwise, between these two, there were many shades of grey, so everything was boiled down to just black or white.[92] Bagchi also believed that Premji was a patriot and worked towards nation-building. This stemmed from Premji's belief that business is a powerful tool for change.

Another aspect of Premji's leadership qualities was that he worked hard at employee retention.[93] It was not only enough to hire great talent, and mentor them, and give them enough freedom to operate, but Premji also worked hard to retain this talent. As a result, Wipro management had people who had been working for a long duration with the company.

Training

Wipro under Azim Premji followed a very strict process of training its people. Given the fact that Wipro was in the IT business, and software technology is a rapidly-evolving field, Wipro gave a lot of importance to training its people.

The practice could have been inspired by Premji himself, who was a keen learner. Premji is known to have a long-lasting and impactful influence on the young executives that he mentors. This influence results in their loyalty and long

---

[92]Subroto Bagchi, 'Patriotic Businessman: Ex-colleague Subroto Bagchi on Azim Premji', The Quint, 13 June 2019, accessed 30 June 2019, https://www.thequint.com/videos/news-videos/subroto-bagchi-on-azim-premji-wipro-chairperson

[93]Bhavya Kaushal, '3 Valuable Entrepreneurial Lessons from India's IT Czar Who Calls It a Day', *Entrepreneur India*, 8 June 2019, accessed 30 June 2019, https://www.entrepreneur.com/slideshow/334994

service to the organization. For instance, Suresh Senapaty stepped down as Wipro's CFO, after a thirty-five-year-long stint with Wipro. Even after this, he remains an advisor to Premji.

There are many Wipro alumni who have gone on to lead their firms or make their mark in the IT sector, in other companies. Some of them have inculcated the habits that they have learnt during their tenure with Wipro.

Premji's leadership style and business ethics have inspired many industry leaders who seek to emulate these in their leadership styles. These were leaders such as Mindtree founders Krishnakumar Natarajan, Rostow Ravanan and Subroto Bagchi.

Suresh Vaswani, the former CEO of Wipro, later led Dell and IBM before launching his venture capital and private equity fund. Natarajan, chairman of Mindtree, had stated, 'In my early days as a campus recruit, I got to know him and observe him...you notice a lot of the ability to become a great professional and you get influenced by some of those actions. This, you then start inculcating in the way you work... He (Azim Premji) is a very tall and respected leader. We have learnt a lot from him when working there... His rigour, detail orientation, precise questioning and the ability to take on difficult issues head-on have always helped many professional managers blossom.'[94]

---

[94]Harish Puppala and Rakesh Sharma, 'Digging Deeper—Azim Premji: The End of an Era', Moneycontrol.com, accessed 30 June 2019, https://www.moneycontrol.com/news/podcast/digging-deeper-azim-premji-the-end-of-an-era-4090341.html

When Premji had announced his retirement, he had sent a letter to all the Wipro personnel. In this letter, he did not take any credit for the success of Wipro, but, in fact, credited the thousands of Wipro employees for shaping and building Wipro into the successful, ethical and socially-responsible organization that it had become.[95]

This was unique in terms of Premji not claiming any credit for the success of Wipro, but instead passing on the complete credit to his employees.

The freedom to operate that he gave is something that all his managers remember. As a leader, Premji placed trust in his colleagues and as long as each colleague did their homework, he backed them up. He was regarded as a professional-minded leader who ran the organization on merit and facts.[96]

A former CEO who had worked in Wipro has been quoted as saying, 'The freedom he gave helped us to become better decision-makers.'[97]

---

[95] Ayan Pramanik and Megha Mandavia, 'That's IT, Over to You Folks: Azim Premji on His Retirement', *The Economic Times*, 7 June 2019, accessed 30 June 2019, https://economictimes.indiatimes.com/tech/ites/thats-it-over-to-you-folks-azim-premji-to-wipro-employees/articleshow/69683892.cms

[96] Dilp Ranjekar, quoted in Ayan Pramanik, Megha Mandavia, 'That's IT, Over to You Folks: Azim Premji on his Retirement', *The Economic Times*, 7 June 2019, accessed 30 June 2019, https://economictimes.indiatimes.com/tech/ites/thats-it-over-to-you-folks-azim-premji-to-wipro-employees/articleshow/69683892.cmshttps://economictimes.indiatimes.com/tech/ites/thats-it-over-to-you-folks-azim-premji-to-wipro-employees/articleshow/69683892.cms

[97] Ayan Pramanik and Megha Mandavia, 'That's IT, Over to You Folks: Azim Premji on His Retirement', *The Economic Times*, 7 June 2019,

Another Wipro campus hire in 1981, K.K. Natarajan, said that he applied Premji's rigour and attention to detail as a great lesson in his journey as a manager. He stated, 'He also gave space to his people. There is nothing you cannot disagree on with Premji. You can disagree with him on a public forum, but once a decision is taken, he doesn't carry anything into a future interaction.'[98]

Besides these examples of managers being given freedom and empowerment, Premji held personal sessions with his managers. He held a session for first-time employees where he explained Wipro's six 'beliefs' (detailed below). He also holds annual communications sessions with all the employees, where he encourages questions and gives sincere answers.[99]

ACCOUNTABILITY AND PERFORMANCE ORIENTATION

On one occasion, in one of the Wipro meetings, an agitated salesperson had complained to Premji that Wipro Systems was buying their computers from Wipro's biggest competitor

---

accessed 30 June 2019, https://economictimes.indiatimes.com/tech/ites/thats-it-over-to-you-folks-azim-premji-to-wipro-employees/articleshow/69683892.cms

[98] Ayan Pramanik and Megha Mandavia, 'That's IT, Over to You Folks: Azim Premji on His Retirement', *The Economic Times*, 7 June 2019, accessed 30 June 2019, https://economictimes.indiatimes.com/tech/ites/thats-it-over-to-you-folks-azim-premji-to-wipro-employees/articleshow/69683892.cms

[99] Kalyan Banerjee, 'Eight Reasons Azim Premji Is Much Bigger Than Just the Sum of His Money', Scroll.in, 4 July 2019, accessed 25 August 2019, https://scroll.in/article/928316/eight-reasons-azim-premji-is-much-bigger-than-just-the-sum-of-his-money

instead of Wipro, expecting some cooperation from him. Premji was, on the contrary, quite clear in his response. He said all businesses were free to decide how to run themselves, and they were free to buy products of their competitors if Wipro products were not comparable.[100]

In another meeting, Premji was told by another Wipro employee about a Wipro finance product performing below expectations. The employee had convinced his father-in-law to invest and hence he was embarrassed at the poor performance, to which Premji stated that they should not recommend Wipro products out of loyalty, and should do so only if they are convinced that the product is the best in the market.[101]

Another incident that occurred in the eighties was related by one of his channel partners in a blog.[102] At the annual two-day Wipro sales channel partner business conference, the channel partners were not happy with the quality of the low-end personal computers (PCs) introduced by Wipro under the brand name 'Popular PC'. The opening session was interrupted by the channel partners who were expressing their dissatisfaction. Premji, who was also present at the conference, delayed the conference, and listened to the concerns of the

---

[100] Kalyan Banerjee, 'Eight Reasons Azim Premji Is Much Bigger Than Just the Sum of His Money', Scroll.in, 4 July 2019, accessed 25 August 2019, https://scroll.in/article/928316/eight-reasons-azim-premji-is-much-bigger-than-just-the-sum-of-his-money
[101] Ibid.
[102] Mahesh Khatri, 'Azim Premji—A Legendary Indian Industrialist Retires Today', 30 July 2019, accessed 25 August 2019, https://medium.com/@MaheshNKhatri/azim-premji-a-legendary-indian-industrialist-retires-today-b65de46cb86e

channel partners patiently. The conference continued after this two-hour session during which Premji took extensive notes along with his top management and teams from the sales, service and production functions. He promised to revert with his answers within the next day's sessions. The first day's sessions ended late in the night, due to the two-hour delay.

The channel partners were pleasantly surprised when, the next day, Premji took the first session to address all their concerns. He also ensured that in case of any commitments, there were fixed time frames with responsibilities assigned to designated individuals. Later, the channel partners discovered that the team, along with Premji, had spent most of the first night in an internal meeting to find solutions for the concerns raised by the channel partners earlier that day.[103]

In another blog post, it is mentioned that Premji, when driving from the Wipro Headquarters at Bengaluru to the Mysore factory, would stop along the way if he happened to see a Wipro lighting outlet. He would introduce himself and take notes based on the feedback about the quality of the products and customer satisfaction.[104]

Wipro's Six Beliefs:

1. Respect the individual
2. Be a business leader

---

[103] Mahesh Khatri, 'Azim Premji—A Legendary Indian Industrialist Retires Today', 30 July 2019, accessed 25 August 2019, https://medium.com/@MaheshNKhatri/azim-premji-a-legendary-indian-industrialist-retires-today-b65de46cb86e
[104] Ibid.

3. Accomplish all tasks in a superior manner
4. Maintain the highest ethical standards
5. Serve customers well
6. Measure performance based on long-term profitability.

These later evolved into a series of guidelines and are codified in their code of business conduct and ethics which now include the following:[105]

Spirit of Wipro

- Be passionate about clients' successes
- Treat each person with respect
- Be global and responsible
- Unyielding integrity in everything we do

LEARNINGS

Azim Premji has followed the principle of getting good people right from the start. At the time he took over his family business, he probably understood the importance of having competent people around to run the business.

We can see how Premji aspired high from the very beginning. Going to hire people from the foremost management institutions (even though initially he did come

---

[105] Wipro.com, accessed 25 August 2019, https://www.wipro.com/content/dam/nexus/en/investor/corporate-governance/policies-and-guidelines/ethical-guidelines/code-of-business-conduct-and-ethics.pdf

back empty-handed), shows his seriousness for getting good talent. This is a very important and critical component for businesses that want to grow. One cannot grow beyond one's capabilities and limitations, and hiring good professionals is the only way one can extend the organizational growth beyond oneself. A logical thought, but this is not something that is commonly followed by most family-owned or founder-driven businesses. In most cases, they would like to stay at the helm as long as possible and would not like to delegate. And this leads to the eventual downfall of organizations that are not able to attract, retain and train good talent. Premji showed wisdom and vision in wanting to hire the best talent, and aiming high. The other aspect of this point is that he did realize that he had limitations since there was competition for talent. The best people wanted to join other companies and even his competitors, rather than work for him. Knowing this fact, he worked on this aspect before trying to attract them. The patience and conviction in his beliefs and transparency of purpose worked for him.

The fact that the alumni have gone on to launch their startups speaks volumes of the high calibre of the Wipro employees.

The story does not end there.

Hiring talent is one part of the story. The other aspect is the retention and training.

Maybe as a result of being in a fast-changing business of IT services, Premji must have realized the importance of having well-trained people. So, it was not just the fact of hiring good people, but continuing to invest in their training. One needs to ensure that this is done to maintain the competitiveness of the firm. Premji made the effort to have open meetings with the first-time employees of the firm. During these meetings, he explained the values of Wipro and also sincerely answered any question asked.

Having the top management meet and answer queries from employees sends out a very strong message. Additionally, meeting them periodically, in an annual meeting, also reinforces the values and the behaviours expected from each one of them. This is a very powerful way to communicate what the organization holds as non-negotiable and what it stands for. (Of course, the people also observe if the CEO or the top man follows what he or she says are the values, but in this case, this was not an issue with Premji, as he was perhaps one of the most authentic leaders living his values!)

His statements of holding his businesses accountable but giving them the freedom to make their decisions, even if that included the freedom to buy the goods of their competitors if they were better, shows maturity on his part to allow his people to make their own decisions. Most often, firms become lazy if they are able to force internal departments to buy the company-made goods. And if these volumes are high, then the internal departments may not have any incentive to be competitive. By forcing these products to be competitive, even for internal business, Premji ensured that different products of the company did not take any business for granted.

His statement for ensuring that even the Wipro employees recommend products only if they are convinced that they are good also increased the accountability and pressure on the

Wipro businesses to be performance-oriented. This was a very smart move, as it forced all the businesses to be competitive.

Even today, most family-run businesses pay very little attention to the training of their teams, which is a short-term measure. The lack of training results in lower productivity for the organization and also lack of any incentives for the people to stay in the firm.

One can hire great people and then even train them extremely well. But if one does not have methods of retaining these people, then organizations will fail, as they will not receive any benefits, but will just become poaching grounds for other companies to attract the best-trained people! So the retention of people is important for organizations to progress. The best people may be highly motivated, but if there are not enough growth opportunities or challenges which give meaning to their jobs, they may just leave. Leaders should never lose sight of the fact that good people will always find good opportunities, and can be highly mobile. Premji operated in an industry that was highly competitive, and had other reputable and comparably-sized competitors. This was an industry which later on attracted some of the biggest technology companies in the world, and all of them were eager to hire good Indian engineers.

Premji faced the tough task of ensuring that his people did not leave for other companies that might have paid much higher than what he was offering. Premji's behaviour towards them was extremely cordial and professional. By ensuring that he had got a good atmosphere for talent to work and thrive, including letting people disagree with him in meetings, he was able to make Wipro an organization where people looked for long-term careers.

Premji also kept the managers accountable and did not hesitate to hold them responsible for their actions. His wanting to ensure that people are committed to solving the issues of customers and to lead from the front serves as an inspiration. It is not every day that we find a CEO willing to listen to consumers and work towards solving the customer's problems. In fact, this is a lesson we can all learn from. How many organizations actively listen to their customers? And even if they listen, what do they do?

We can estimate the significance of this question, if one were to ask how often an organization solicits the opinions of customers. In fact, in some organizations, the firms go out of their way to avoid being contacted by the customers or treat them badly and then put barriers of call centres or websites without any information on how to contact them. Such organizations often face the wrath of the customers, who would choose to take their business to the competition the first chance they get.

Premji actively sought feedback from his customers and his channel partners. In fact, many people have remarked on his curiosity to find out how Wipro was doing and taking copious notes. His responsiveness and willingness to give a patient hearing to all and then, addressing the problems and making a time-bound plan for those concerns not met immediately, is refreshing to read about. His care for the customers' issues illustrates that he understood the fact that revenues eventually do come from the customer, hence one should pay close attention to their complaints instead of avoiding them. This is also a very mature viewpoint, as it is only when one gets undiluted and honest feedback that one can improve and get a realistic picture of where one stands and what the reality in the market is. Usually, the higher up one is in the organization, the more difficult it is to get this information accurately and timely. As 'gatekeepers' in the form of executives, employees may filter out the information and only feed what information they would want to convey to their leaders. Hence it is always advisable for the senior management to conduct these surveys by themselves, so that they know first-hand what the customers really think. This is similar to Emperor Akbar walking in disguise amongst his people at night to find out what his subjects' concerns were. Thus, unadulterated feedback is what the people at the top should ensure is available to them. Because, only then does the true picture of the marketplace emerge.

Leaders should keep in mind that people leave managers and not organizations. Every leader's main task should be to work on getting the best people they can, and then working on creating an organization where they can work unhindered. Premji did this, and the results are there for all to see.

10

MAKE AN IMPACT WITH THE WEALTH THAT YOU GIVE AWAY

We collectively, as a family, very much share a passion and focus on philanthropy... We all feel very unfairly privileged and we feel it is our responsibility to partake and contribute.

—Rishad Premji, in an interview in 2017[106]

I strongly believe that those of us who are privileged to have wealth should contribute significantly to try to create a better world for the millions who are far less privileged.

—Azim Premji[107]

---

[106] Varun Sood, 'Wipro's Rishad Premji: Start-ups Can Do for India What IT Did in Late 1990s', Livemint, 15 September 2017, accessed 4 October 2019, https://www.livemint.com/Companies/UijX0qmHBPdbi9a7OLGfOM/Wipros-Rishad-Premji-Startups-can-do-for-India-what-IT-di.html

[107] Podcast, 'Digging Deep—giving and Growing: The Story of Wipro &

'I became convinced that markets, public systems and philanthropic initiatives, all had a significant role to play if the country was to have inclusive development, and that we needed to work purposefully towards establishing a more humane, equitable and ethical society for all our citizens.'

—Azim Premji, in a letter dated 19 February 2013[108]

CONCEPT OF STEWARDSHIP

The concept of stewardship means that one believes that they are the caretakers of wealth and that they need to preserve, protect and use the wealth for the good of the society and not for personal benefit. Therefore, the efforts of all those who are in possession of wealth need to be channelized towards societal benefits. Premji believed in this concept of stewardship, and he spoke about this in his letter to the shareholders in the 2018–2019 Annual Report (Annexure 4).

Azim Premji's donations alone accounted for more than 80 per cent of the total individual philanthropic contributions

---

Azim Premji', Moneycontrol.com, accessed 30 June 2019, https://www.moneycontrol.com/news/business/companies/podcast-digging-deep-giving-and-growing-the-story-of-wipro-azim-premji-2660341.html
[108]Varun Sood, 'Azim Premji's Charitable Trusts Grow Richer On Dividends, Share Sales', *Livemint*, 18 March 2019, accessed 30 June 2019, https://www.livemint.com/companies/people/azim-premji-s-charitable-trusts-grow-richer-on-dividends-share-sales-1552846750940.html

Make an Impact with the Wealth That You Give Away   81

in India in 2018.[109] This is at a time when the rate of philanthropic contributions in India is rising, with contributions of ₹10 crore or more, comprising more than 50 per cent of the total individual philanthropy.

Bill Gates, the tech billionaire, co-founder of Microsoft, said in a tweet on the social media platform Twitter, 'I'm inspired by Azim Premji's continued commitment to philanthropy. His latest contribution will make a tremendous impact'. This was at the time Premji announced his generous contribution.

'He has been most successful in creating a very successful IT company. However, the greatest legacy he has passed on to the corporate world is philanthropy. He does not throw his wealth around and has a very simple living and has shown that the wealth does not always have to go to the family and can be given to the charitable cause,' said Anu Aga, chairperson, Thermax, the Pune-based engineering firm.[110]

Andrew Carnegie, the American self-made steel magnate, first propagated the idea that wealthy individuals must give away their money to society instead of keeping it in the family.

Carnegie had started giving away his money at the age of thirty-five. By the time he died, in 1919, he had given away more than 90 per cent of his wealth. His book, *The Gospel*

---

[109] Kalpana Pathak, 'Azim Premji Raises Philanthropy Bar with $21 Billion Total Pledge', *Livemint*, 13 March 2019, accessed 30 June 2019, https://www.livemint.com/companies/people/azim-premji-raises-philanthropy-bar-with-21-billion-total-pledge-1552500208294.html

[110] Varun Sood and Sundeep Khanna, 'Making of Azim Premji: The Philanthropist', *Livemint*, 24 June 2019, accessed 28 June 2019, https://www.livemint.com/companies/people/making-of-azim-premji-the-philanthropist-1561390035003.html

of Wealth, which he wrote in 1889, proposed his ideas for the best use of wealth. In it, he stated that the best use of surplus wealth was not extravagant expenditure or personal indulgence, but to give it back for society's welfare. He also encouraged the government to tax such wealth transfers very heavily.[111] Premji seems to be following this belief of giving away his wealth for the betterment of society.

No story on Premji can be complete if it does not mention the philanthropic initiatives that he has undertaken.

Azim Premji has set up two philanthropic trusts—Azim Premji Philanthropic Initiatives Private Limited (APPI), earlier called the Azim Premji Foundation,[112] and Azim Premji Trust (APT).

The Azim Premji Foundation was founded in 2001 with an aim to make long-term contribution to education in India.[113] It was set up as a not-for-profit Foundation, with a vision of enhancing quality and equity in the public school education system in India, to build a better society, with an endowment

---

[111] Aakar Patel, 'Azim Premji to Hang Up His Boots: Wipro Chairman Led a Modest Life, Set Example for Other Billionaires to Give Up Surplus Wealth', Firstpost.com, 10 June 2019, accessed 29 June 2019, https://www.firstpost.com/business/azim-premji-to-hang-up-his-boots-wipro-chairman-led-a-modest-life-set-example-for-other-billionaires-to-give-up-surplus-wealth-6783971.html

[112] Varun Sood, 'Azim Premji Trusts Get a Share of His Wealth, but Not Voting Rights', *Livemint*, 19 March 2019, accessed 30 June 2019, https://www.livemint.com/companies/news/azim-premji-trusts-get-a-share-of-his-wealth-but-not-voting-rights-1552935688818.html

[113] Azim Premji Foundation, accessed 23 September 2019, https://azimpremjifoundation.org/tags/organization

of Wipro shares worth $125 million.[114] Premji had subsequently followed up with donations worth more than $4 billion.

The Azim Premji Foundation works to improve access to primary education in India, including some of its most disadvantaged parts. The Foundation trains many thousands of teachers in seven states, covering nearly fifty districts. The purpose of focusing on teachers is to ensure that the standard of education in government schools is raised, and the quality of education to the students in these schools rises.[115] Premji's philanthropic initiatives also help in improving the lives of street children and the disabled.[116]

In 2014, Premji set up APPI, a grant-making body on the lines of the Bill and Melinda Gates Foundation, intending to give grants to non-governmental organizations. The shares in Wipro held by the Azim Premji Foundation were transferred to APPI.

APPI supports not-for-profits through financial grants, which work in areas of human development complementing education, such as nutrition, local governance, and well-being of vulnerable groups.[117] The main aim of APPI is to

---

[114] Ajim H. Premji, Wipro.com, accessed 29 June 2019, https://www.wipro.com/en-IN/leadership/azim-h-premji/

[115] Varun Sood and Sundeep Khanna, 'Making of Azim Premji: The Philanthropist', *Livemint*, 24 June 2019, accessed 28 June 2019, https://www.livemint.com/companies/people/making-of-azim-premji-the-philanthropist-1561390035003.html

[116] Kalpana Pathak, 'Azim Premji Raises Philanthropy Bar with USD$21 Billion Total Pledge', Livemint, 13 March 2019, accessed 30 June 2019, https://www.livemint.com/companies/people/azim-premji-raises-philanthropy-bar-with-21-billion-total-pledge-1552500208294.html34

[117] Azim H. Premji, Wipro.com, accessed 29 June 2019, https://www.

donate ₹500 crore every year to non-profits who work for the underserved groups of society, like the street children and the disabled. APPI also works to promote governance.[118] The earnings of these two trusts (APPI and APT) go into the Azim Premji Endowment Fund (APEF), which releases funds for philanthropic projects.[119] The endowment owns 14 per cent of the promoters' shareholding in Wipro, and in March 2019, Premji transferred the 53 per cent economic stake to the endowment (that means the dividends earned by these 53 per cent shares). The fund has an endowment valued at $21 billion, making it one of the largest private endowments in the world.[120]

The trusts, however, have been staying away from voting on any resolutions relating to Wipro, and are also not able to nominate any members to Wipro's Board.[121] Hence this would ensure that the trusts, by virtue of being the largest economic beneficiaries, do not influence any matter on the Wipro Board and hence the Board can work independently of them.

---

wipro.com/en-IN/leadership/azim-h-premji/

[118] Arunadhati Ramanathan, 'Premji's Trusts Gain Rs 1900 Crore Via Share Repurchase by Wipro', 21 July 2016, accessed 30 June 2019, https://www.livemint.com/

[119] 'Azim Premji's Charitable Trusts Among The Richest in India', *Forbes India*, 18 March 2019, accessed 30 June 2019, http://www.forbesindia.com/news/business/azim-premjis-charitable-trusts-among-the-richest-in-india-3658881.html

[120] Varun Sood, 'Azim Premji's Charitable Trusts Grow Richer on Dividends, Share Sales', *Livemint*, 18 March 2019, accessed 30 June 2019, https://www.livemint.com/companies/people/azim-premji-s-charitable-trusts-grow-richer-on-dividends-share-sales-1552846750940.html

[121] Ibid.

Make an Impact with the Wealth That You Give Away   85

This fund releases the money for all the philanthropic work done by the two trusts. The Foundation has been scaling up its activities to cover more than forty districts in six states, and the philanthropic arm has been issuing grants to non-government organizations, besides founding the Azim Premji University.

Anurag Behar, CEO of the Azim Premji Foundation, had stated in a newspaper article that Premji had got influenced by observing his mother's work for more than fifty years, and by the concept of trusteeship of wealth, an idea proposed by Mahatma Gandhi.[122] These ideas germinated into seeds for pursuing philanthropy, and for the Foundation, as early as 1999–2000 itself.[123]

The spirit of doing good for society was always running in the family. Azim Premji's mother, Gulbanoo M.H. Hasham Premji, was a trained doctor who set up a children's orthopaedic charitable hospital at Haji Ali in Mumbai. She has been reported to have spent a lifetime helping to set up this hospital,[124] right from when she was twenty-seven years old till the age of seventy-seven![125] Azim Premji recalled that they

---

[122] Varun Sood and Sundeep Khanna, 'Making of Azim Premji: The Philanthropist', *Livemint*, 24 June 2019, accessed 28 June 2019, https://www.livemint.com/companies/people/making-of-azim-premji-the-philanthropist-1561390035003.html

[123] Ibid.

[124] Ibid.

[125] Anil Dharkar, 'Bhaskar Interview: Joh Sampann Hai, Unhe Garibo Ke Behtar Jeevan Ke Liye Kuch Na Kuch Karna Chahiye: Azim Premji,' *Dainik Bhaskar*, 29 July 2019, accessed 25 August 2019, https://www.bhaskar.com/national/news/wipro-chairman-azim-premji-retires-01605177.html

did not have much money and his mother had to work very hard to arrange funds. They had approached the government for help. The government announced the funds but they had to spend all their time in trying to get the funds released. He recalls his mother working for nine hours every day, in spite of the fact that there were already four children in the family.[126] Her dedication to this cause remained, even as she was serving as the chairperson of Wipro after her husband passed away in August 1966.[127] As I stated earlier, the roots of serving society run deep in the Premji family.

Azim Premji first thought of this idea around 2000. Even the thought of setting up a charitable foundation was discussed thoroughly with the executives who would be running it before it took its first steps.[128]

Azim Premji felt that the wealthy should do something to improve the lives of the poor. He felt that the mandatory limit set up by the government for corporates to spend 2 per cent of their profits every year towards Corporate Social Responsibility (CSR) projects was not helping, as many corporates had been giving the funds to their own foundations only. This was a practice which he felt should be stopped. He

---

[126] Anil Dharkar, 'Bhaskar Interview: Joh Sampann Hai, Unhe Garibo Ke Behtar Jeevan Ke Liye Kuch Na Kuch Karna Chahiye: Azim Premji', *Dainik Bhaskar*, 29 July 2019, accessed 25 August 2019, https://www.bhaskar.com/national/news/wipro-chairman-azim-premji-retires-01605177.html
[127] Varun Sood and Sundeep Khanna, 'Making of Azim Premji: The Philanthropist', *Livemint*, 24 June 2019, accessed 28 June 2019, https://www.livemint.com/companies/people/making-of-azim-premji-the-philanthropist-1561390035003.html
[128] Ibid.

gave the example of Wipro, where no part of their CSR fund of ₹400 crores was given to their own Wipro Foundation.[129]

The various areas where the proposed foundation's efforts could focus on were discussed. And four areas were shortlisted. These areas—education, nutrition, healthcare and governance—were possible sectors where their efforts could be directed. However, after further discussions, primary education was finally chosen. The rationale for choosing primary education over all the other areas was that, while they felt it was clear there were other important areas where they could work, the education sector had a fundamental characteristic, which swung their decision in its favour. They concluded that it was education that was the most important way for empowering people.[130]

Additionally, Premji did not want to just issue a cheque and do it as a way to convince himself that he had done some good, according to an executive.[131] Instead, his vision was guided by the realization that any efforts had to bring out large-scale change or at least start the process of transformation, for any philanthropic efforts to be meaningful.[132] Premji took a deep

---

[129] Anil Dharkar, 'Bhaskar Interview: Joh Sampann Hai, Unhe Garibo Ke Behtar Jeevan Ke Liye Kuch Na Kuch Karna Chahiye: Azim Premji', *Dainik Bhaskar*, 29 July 2019, accessed 25 August 2019, https://www.bhaskar.com/national/news/wipro-chairman-azim-premji-retires-01605177.html
[130] Varun Sood and Sundeep Khanna, 'Making of Azim Premji: The Philanthropist', *Livemint*, 24 June 2019, accessed 28 June 2019, https://www.livemint.com/companies/people/making-of-azim-premji-the-philanthropist-1561390035003.html
[131] Ibid.
[132] Varun Sood and Sundeep Khanna, 'Making of Azim Premji: The Philanthropist', *Livemint*, 24 June 2019, accessed 28 June 2019, https://

interest in the activities of the Foundation, beyond just setting it up, which included him being hands-on to a large extent, including frequent visits to schools in remote areas so that he could get an idea of the activities first-hand.

Azim Premji started working with government schools to understand and learn about the education system. He went to some schools in the rural areas and spent some time with the teachers and principals to get a first-hand idea of the ground realities that existed there. He understood the extraordinary complexities and challenges that the teachers faced. And he saw the commitment that they demonstrated in the face of these challenges. He then realized that it was education that would shape our society, and the frontline of good and committed teachers would determine the success of our education system. But our society had, over the past decades, systematically undervalued and underinvested in our teachers. He realized that the BEd programme (the educational programme for training teachers) needed to be overhauled. The existing nine million teachers supported and empowered society and society must stop blaming teachers for the gaps in our education system.[133]

Azim Premji went on to state:

'We must give them (the teachers) their due place in society as the architects and developers of a good society. They must

---

www.livemint.com/companies/people/making-of-azim-premji-the-philanthropist-1561390035003.html

[133] Azim Premji, 'Don't Blame the Teacher: Azim Premji', 26 April 2018, accessed 30 June 2019, https://www.indiatoday.in/magazine/guest-column/story/20180507-azim-premji-column-on-indian-education-system-teachers-1221665-2018-04-26

be empowered, trusted and supported. This requires a cultural revolution in our education system and society at large.

'The progress of India will be determined by the capacity and motivation of the front line in all fields of human development. We must invest in and value the front line. We have not done this till now, so it needs urgent and dramatic change. Human capacity in the front line, supported by an empowering culture, is the crux of making our country more just, equitable, humane and sustainable. We must put all our national might behind this.'[134]

The Foundation runs the Azim Premji University, which was established in 2010 by an act of the Karnataka Legislative Assembly. The objectives are to run programmes to develop education and development professionals, offer alternative models for educational change and also invest in educational research.[135]

When he announced his intention to step down, Premji was preparing for his second innings to devote to his other passion, the philanthropic arm. It was quoted that Premji's unrelenting questioning and ability to drill down to the basic details of every transaction would serve as a huge benefit for the Foundation. The Foundation, at the time, in June 2019, had been operating for more than eighteen years, with an excellent team at the helm, that had been handpicked by Premji, and

---

[134] Azim Premji, 'Don't Blame the Teacher: Azim Premji', 26 April 2018, accessed 30 June 2019, https://www.indiatoday.in/magazine/guest-column/story/20180507-azim-premji-column-on-indian-education-system-teachers-1221665-2018-04-26

[135] Azim Premji Foundation, accessed 30 June 2019, https://azimpremjifoundation.org/tags/organization

had adequate funds to ensure that they were not dependent on dipping into the fortunes of Wipro (since their major source of funding is from the financial dividends of Wipro).[136]

FUNDING OF THE FOUNDATION

The Foundation was started with an initial endowment of Wipro shares worth about $125 million in 2001. Over the years, between 2001 and 2019, Azim Premji donated Wipro shares worth around $12 billion to the Foundation. This included the announcement made by him in early 2019, where he transferred the economic ownership of 34 per cent of his shares in Wipro, worth approximately $7.5 billion, to the Azim Premji Philanthropic Initiatives and the Azim Premji Trust.[137] Today the Foundation has an endowment of $21 billion, which is amongst the top five endowments anywhere in the world.[138] This was with the economic interest of 53 per cent promoters which was transferred to the Foundation in 2019. This was in addition to the 14 per cent stake that it already had. The balance 7 per cent was with Azim Premji, his wife Yasmeen, and two sons, Rishad and Tariq.[139]

As mentioned earlier, the Foundation has 67 per cent of the economic interests of Wipro's shareholding (that is, it

---

[136]Varun Sood and Sundeep Khanna, 'Making of Azim Premji: The Philanthropist', *Livemint*, 24 June 2019, accessed 28 June 2019, https://www.livemint.com/companies/people/making-of-azim-premji-the-philanthropist-1561390035003.html
[137]Ibid.
[138]Ibid.
[139]Ibid.

is entitled to all the dividends and financial benefits of the shares, except the voting rights, which belong to Premji). The Foundation has earned around ₹11,357 crores over the last nine years, on account of the dividends, share sales and buybacks. This has made it amongst the richest and largest charitable trusts in India.

The Foundation also gets returns from Azim Premji's family office, PremjiInvest. Reported sources state that the family office is managing funds amounting to about $5 billion to $7 billion and has delivered returns of above 30 per cent over the last two years.

In 2013, Azim Premji became the first Indian billionaire to sign the Giving Pledge, an initiative by Bill Gates and Warren Buffet. This initiative encourages wealthy individuals to pledge half their fortunes to philanthropy.[140] Premji has given much more than what the pledge required and the size of his generosity has been compared to the contributions made by the Tatas historically.[141]

The Foundation is run by Anurag Behar and Dileep Ranjekar, co-chief executive officers, who had been associated with Wipro earlier, in different capacities.

---

[140]'Why India's Rich Don't Give Their Money Away', BBC News, 2 April 2019, accessed 30 June 2019, https://www.bbc.com/news/world-asia-india-47566542
[141]Ibid.

WORKING OF THE FOUNDATION[142]

The Azim Premji Foundation was established in 2001 to ensure sustainable improvement in elementary education in rural clusters in India by training teachers, administrators and educational functionaries.

By 2019, the Foundation had been working in seven states with more than 350,000 schools.[143] It works in states such as Karnataka, Chhattisgarh, Madhya Pradesh, Telangana, Rajasthan and Uttarakhand, and the union territory of Puducherry. In 2019,[144] the Foundation had its presence in more than forty-seven districts in six states through a network of field institutes. Besides, it also has special-focus schools in at least six backward districts, a varsity in Bengaluru, and other non-profit partners. The Foundation had been providing grants to around 150 NGOs for projects ranging from three to five years in duration, covering areas like supporting differently-abled people and orphans, drug abuse control, violence against women, trafficking, and more. It was estimated that the annual grants given by the Foundation were more than ₹100 crore at the time.

PremjiInvest, the family office of Azim Premji, is India's biggest family office, managing assets worth at least $3 billion. It focuses on private equity and venture capital

---

[142]Yuvraj Malik, 'Azim Premji Foundation to Scale Up Fieldwork, Increase Grants', *Business Standard*, 15 March 2019, accessed 30 June 2019, https://www.business-standard.com/article/companies/azim-premji-foundation-to-scale-up-fieldwork-increase-grants-119031401358_1.html
[143]Ibid.
[144]Ibid.

investments. Currently, PremjiInvest has invested in, and holds stakes in, companies like Marico, HDFC, Aditya Birla Capital, Snapdeal, Flipkart, FabIndia and Lenskart to name a few.[145] In March 2018, he merged the family office investment arm, PremjiInvest, with Azim Premji Trust, the holding entity for the endowment trusts that he had set up in 2001.[146] This effectively meant that Premji wanted to give away more to charity, with the $3 billion investment assets under PremjiInvest also being added to the $9 billion endowment funds, totalling about $12 billion.[147]

Ravi Venkatesan, a former head of Microsoft India and a major proponent of philanthropy, has said, 'We need to move from a mindset of spare change to real change. So, while charitable giving is still important, more funding must go towards systemic solutions to major problems such as literacy, healthcare, livelihoods, etc. Philanthropy must be more strategic and more collaborative.'[148]

---

[145] 'Happy Birthday Azim Premji! Did You Know These Five Facts About the Wipro Chairman?' Timesnownews.com, 24 July 2018, accessed 30 June 2019, https://www.timesnownews.com/business-economy/companies/article/happy-birthday-azim-premji-did-you-know-these-five-facts-about-wipro-chairman/258930

[146] Pankaj Mishra, 'Azim Premji Quietly Gives Away More to Charity', Livemint, 7 March 2019, accessed 30 June 2019, https://www.livemint.com/Companies/6fd1boxRbPYAuRoeNk852L/Azim-Premji-quietly-gives-away-more-to-charity.html

[147] Ibid.

[148] Ibid.

LEARNINGS

Azim Premji has earned money the good old-fashioned way, by hard work and integrity. He did not take shortcuts, ensuring that the strictest governance processes were followed for his company, which stood for integrity and honesty.

He devoted his wealth to charitable causes, helping to uplift society and to make an impact in areas that needed to be supported. His philanthropic causes have helped to make an impact on society.

In his choosing to donate a significant part of his wealth to this cause, he has ensured that the good work carries on, on a sustainable basis.

'Azim Premji's commitment to philanthropy, which began with the cause of education for disadvantaged children, has been a strong message to corporations and businessmen. His recent commitment will contribute towards meeting his vision of inclusive development,' said Ratan Tata, Chairman Emeritus, Tata Sons.[149]

The fact that the Foundation is run professionally, and has its own source of independent funding, shows the foresight of Azim Premji. This way, the Foundation can work effectively without being dependent on any external influences such as donors who may put conditions on donations, or having to make any choices that would prevent it from following the path it has set out for itself.

---

[149]Varun Sood and Sundeep Khanna, 'Making of Azim Premji: The Philanthropist', *Livemint*, 24 June 2019, accessed 28 June 2019, https://www.livemint.com/companies/people/making-of-azim-premji-the-philanthropist-1561390035003.html

Make an Impact with the Wealth That You Give Away 95

It is also pertinent to draw a parallel to the Tatas, where a similar structure is present, where the Tata Trusts own 66 per cent of the Tata Sons, the holding company of the Tata Group. The trusts earn the dividends and have the right to appoint up to three directors on the Tata Sons Board. The trusts can also appoint the chairman of the group holding company. The income in the various trusts is, however, also used for philanthropic and charitable purposes.[150] In the case of Wipro, Premji is chairman of the two trusts and Wipro, whereas in the Tatas, the chairman's posts are occupied by different people.

Premji has earned his wealth fairly and with integrity. He has then chosen to give his wealth away for education. This has been a step that has demonstrated the good that capitalism can do.

I think that there have been numerous previous examples of rich industrialists who have given away wealth, but this has often been tainted either by doubts on the integrity of the wealth creation, or into the areas towards which the largesse is directed. No one has raised any objections to the wealth created by Azim Premji. By ensuring the strictest standards of integrity for his company while creating the wealth, and for ensuring a deep impactful area such as education, which positively influences everyone affected, Premji has ensured that he has created an impact which will long be remembered,

---

[150]Varun Sood, 'Azim Premji Trusts Get a Share of His Wealth, but Not Voting Rights', *Livemint*, 19 March 2019, accessed 30 June 2019, https://www.livemint.com/companies/news/azim-premji-trusts-get-a-share-of-his-wealth-but-not-voting-rights-1552935688818.html

if not for the size, then for the impact that it has had, for years to come. It is a relief for the recluse billionaire who had preferred to remain away from the spotlight that he has contributed his billions to an area, that will carry on doing his work, just like he was—quietly, efficiently and behind the scenes.

What kind of business leaders does India need?

The answer is simple. It needs many more business leaders like Azim Premji.

This is because Azim Premji has never been just a bystander. He is a catalyst. And a doer. A game-changer. And this time, he has set out to change lives and to be a trustee of wealth, rather than just its owner.[151]

---

[151] Podcast, 'Digging Deep—Giving and Growing: The Story of Wipro and Azim Premji', Moneycontrol.com, accessed 30 June 2019, https://www.moneycontrol.com/news/business/companies/podcast-digging-deep-giving-and-growing-the-story-of-wipro-azim-premji-2660341.html

11
SUMMARY OF LEARNINGS

Azim Premji inherited a groundnut oil business, which he was asked to take over, right in the middle of his studies at Stanford. This was in 1966 when his father passed away. The Western India Vegetable Products Limited was a listed company on the Bombay Stock Exchange, and had revenues of about $3 million, and Premji's family owned about 50 per cent of the company.

Premji took over and changed the fortunes of his family business, and today, Wipro is amongst the top three IT companies in India. Additionally, it has created huge wealth for all its shareholders. This made Premji amongst the wealthiest people in India.

Premji had about 74 per cent of the total equity, preferring to buy shares from the dividends that the company used to give annually. In 2019, he announced that he would be giving away a total of 67 per cent of his shares to a family foundation, which would use the funds for philanthropy. This total quantum of $21 billion is amongst the largest endowments ever given for philanthropy in the world.

Let us summarize what we learn from his journey and what we have seen in the earlier chapters:

HUMILITY

Azim Premji is a very humble person, low-key and media-shy. He tries to stay away from the spotlight, and prefers to carry on doing his work, without getting too bothered about media coverage or publicity.

HARD WORK

Azim Premji works hard, often getting to work early. He is regarded as a positive influence on the people around him, hence serves as an example for others to emulate. He does not hesitate to 'get his hands dirty' and do the work himself.

INTEGRITY

Azim Premji has been maintaining a very high degree of integrity and is not willing to accept any violation of these principles. He is known to have fired employees who may have shown lack of integrity, regardless of the fact that the amount involved was trivial. He demands the same level of integrity from all his employees, thus making his company one of the rare cases where integrity is non-negotiable, and this is strictly adhered to.

CORPORATE GOVERNANCE AND TRUSTEESHIP

In the midst of all this wealth, Azim Premji considers himself a custodian of the wealth and not the owner, even though he has created all of it. He considers himself a trustee of the wealth, with the purpose that the wealth needs to be used for social good. This is what drives him, to create profits so that more can be given away to philanthropic causes.

FRUGALNESS

Azim Premji's frugality is well known in the industry. He is aware that he is competing in a cost-conscious industry and hence all wastage would be detrimental to profits. When the profits are being used for philanthropy, then there is a vested interest to increase the profits.

His personal habits of frugality and simple living are transferred to Wipro, so that now everyone in Wipro is cost-conscious.

DEDICATION TO VALUES

Integrity, respect and hard work are values that Premji has been living by. These values are what Premji considers sacrosanct. These are made clear to anyone joining Wipro, hence he is able to attract and retain stakeholders around him, who also consider these values as something they can live by, and would like to adhere to.

KEEP YOUR EYES OPEN TO OPPORTUNITIES TO DIVERSIFY

Azim Premji had been working on his vegetable oil business when he saw an opportunity to enter the hardware industry, and later, the software industry. His story is of his recognizing the opportunities and grabbing them, whether in hardware manufacturing, software development or switching over to Design and R&D for his customers. He did not rest on his laurels and was always open to newer areas for growth.

MEASURE WHAT NEEDS TO BE DONE AND USE TECHNOLOGY FOR GREATER EFFICIENCIES

Azim Premji used systems based on technology to remove subjectivity in his management processes. He used all the advantages that technology gave, to reduce costs and increase profits. This is a good learning that managers can use in their daily work, by asking: Can I use technology to do this work better, cheaper or faster?

ALWAYS LEARN

Azim Premji was always learning. He was in the IT sector, which has a very rapid pace of change, and yet he was humble enough to realize that he needed to learn newer aspects of his job to work better, since he did not know everything. He did not hesitate to seek out experts in various domains and work with them.

HIRE GOOD PEOPLE, TRAIN THEM WELL AND EMPOWER THEM

Azim Premji was always interested in hiring good people, sometimes sitting in at the interviews himself. He took a lot of care in hiring the right people since he was aware from the first day itself that he needed good people if he was to grow. He also focused a lot on their training, and ensured that the people were always trained well and given their freedom and responsibility so that they could operate.

His care for the people built up loyalty and he was able to retain them for a long time, in an industry where the demand for good people outstrips the supply.

USE WEALTH FOR SOCIETAL BENEFITS

Azim Premji created enormous wealth due to the success of Wipro. He gave away a large part of his fortune to philanthropy in a quiet manner, without any fanfare. His gift was not just a knee-jerk reaction, but a result of a well-thought-out plan on how it could be used to achieve a large-scale impact on society. He could have just signed a cheque and the matter would have ended there. But he chose to create a foundation through which it is spent efficiently, to achieve its desired goals. He chose to step down from his business role, to don the philanthropy hat, and to carry on working on his second passion. What results he gets there, we need to wait and see. But if his track record is any indication, it will be done quietly, without any fanfare, hugely impactful, and worth waiting for.

ANNEXURE I

Other global large endowments are as under:[152]

Bill Gates and Melinda Gates Foundation	USA	$51.6 billion
Stichting INGKA Foundation	Netherlands	$36 billion
Wellcome Trust (capital of Sir Henry Wellcome)	London, UK	$27.1 billion
Howard Hughes Medical Institute	USA	$23.8 billion
Garfield Weston Foundation	London, UK	$15.7 billion

---

[152] Shelley Singh, Lijee Philip and Hari Pulakkat, 'How Premji Is Rewriting the Art of Giving', *Economic Times*, 26 March 2019, accessed 30 June 2019, https://economictimes.indiatimes.com/news/company/corporate-trends/catalyst-for-social-change-in-india-taking-the-azim-premji-way/articleshow/68571154.cms

Indian philanthropists:

Shiv Nadar	HCL	$558 million
Kiran Mazumdar-Shaw	Biocon	75 per cent of her wealth
Nandan and Rohini Nilekani	Infosys	50 per cent of their wealth
P.N.C. Menon	Sobha Developers	50 per cent of an estimated $435 million

ANNEXURE 2

Milestones of Wipro:[153]

1945	Incorporation of Wipro, Inc. as a cooking oil company, Western India Vegetable Products Ltd, in Amalner, Maharashtra
1946	Company goes public
1966	After his father, Mohamed Hasham Premji's death, Azim Premji, when he is twenty-one, comes back from Stanford University and takes charge as the company's chairman
1981	Wipro changes focus and concentrated on the booming technology industry
1982	Entry into IT products business
1989	Establishes a joint venture with GE

---

[153]ET Bureau, 'Such a long journey: Azim Premji and Wipro', 7 June 2019, accessed 4 October 2019, https://economictimes.indiatimes.com/tech/ites/such-a-long-journey-azim-premji-and-wipro/articleshow/69684117.cms)

1990	Enters into third party R&D services and IT services
1995	Premji starts taking correspondence classes to complete his engineering degree from Stanford
2000	Listed on the NYSE and enters the BPO business
2002	Company becomes fastest wealth creator in five years (1997-2002 BPO business)
2004	Achieves $1 billion in revenue
2008	Company appoints Girish Paranjpe and Suresh Vaswani as co-CEOs
2011	Experiment with co-CEOs fails; T.K. Kurien elevated as CEO
2013	Demerges its diversified businesses into a separate company, as Wipro Enterprises Ltd. Wipro Ltd to focus exclusively on IT business
2015	Launches 'Wipro Digital'. Key capabilities acquired through DesignIt and Appirio
2016	Abidali Neemuchwala takes over as CEO; Kurien retires
2016	Acquires HealthPlan Services, a technology and business process, as a service provider in the US health insurance market
2016	Ranks 755th on the Forbes Global 2000 list
2017	Launches New Brand Identity and rearticulated 'Spirit of Wipro' to underscore Wipro's commitment to transformation and evolving client expectations
2018	Loses the tag of third-largest IT services firm to rival HCL Technologies
2019	Azim Premji announces his decision to step down as chairman and MD.

ANNEXURE 3

About Azim Premji

(from Wipro.com)

Azim Premji, a graduate in electrical engineering from Stanford University, US, has been at the helm of Wipro Limited since the late 1960s, turning what was then a $2 million hydrogenated cooking fat company into a close to $8.5 billion IT, BPO and R&D services organization with a presence in fifty-eight countries, which it is today. Other companies of the Wipro group led by Premji have revenues of close to $2 billion, spanning successful businesses across consumer goods, precision engineering and healthcare systems.

Premji has been driven by one fundamental business idea—to build an organization deeply committed to values with the client as the focus of all efforts. Unflinching commitment to values continues to remain at the core of Wipro. Premji strongly believes that ordinary people are capable of extraordinary things when organized into highly charged teams.

Wipro's success has been driven by its cutting-edge expertise in technology and understanding of global industries, which deliver real business value to its clients innovatively and consistently. This innovation and consistency is driven by its pioneering efforts in technology, service quality and predictability.

Premji firmly believes that businesses have a deep responsibility to employ ethical, fair and ecologically sensitive business practices, and also to actively engage with fundamental societal issues. Wipro's deep and focused social and environmental initiatives span the countries across its operational footprint, leading to Wipro being recognized as a global leader in sustainability.

In 2001, Premji established the Azim Premji Foundation, a not-for-profit organization, to enhance the quality and equity in the public school education system in India, and to build a better society. The Foundation works in seven states of India which have more than 350,000 schools. It also runs the Azim Premji University, which is focused on teaching and research programmes in education and other areas of human development. Azim Premji Philanthropic Initiatives supports not-for-profits, through financial grants, which work in areas of human development, complementing education, such as nutrition, local governance and well-being of vulnerable groups. Premji's donations to the endowment of the Foundation, at $15 billion, make it one of the largest foundations in the world.

Over the years, Premji has received numerous honours and accolades, which he considers as recognitions for the team of Wipro and the Foundation. *Business Week* listed him amongst the top 30 entrepreneurs in world history. *Financial Times*, *Time*, *Fortune* and *Forbes* have all named him as of one the most influential people in the world, citing his leadership in business and philanthropy, including the contributions to improving public education. *The Journal of Foreign Policy* has listed him amongst the top global thinkers. Premji was also given the Lifetime Achievement Award by the *Economic Times*.

The first Indian recipient of the Faraday Medal, Premji has also been conferred honorary doctorates by Michigan State University and Wesleyan University (in the US), and the Indian Institutes of Technology at Mumbai, Roorkee and Kharagpur, amongst others. The Republic of France has conferred upon him their highest civilian award, 'Knight of the Legion of Honor'. In January 2011, he was conferred with the Padma Vibhushan, the second-highest civilian award in India. In 2017, he was awarded the Carnegie Medal of Philanthropy, which hails the 'conscience, integrity, and compassion that have guided his visionary giving...(with) invaluable benefit to both the nation and to the world'.

ANNEXURE 4

Mr Azim Premji's letter to the shareholders of Wipro, at the last annual general meeting (AGM) that he held as the chairman and managing director of Wipro, just before he stepped down on 20 July 2019.[154]

Dear Stakeholders,

This year, we embark on our 75th year of creating value for our stakeholders. It is an important milestone for us and we take great pride in how Wipro is an exemplar of a successful, ethical and a socially responsible organization. If we look back at the Wipro journey in the last seven decades, from a small vegetable oil company to a leading information technology company that we are today, we have evolved by constantly

---

[154]'Outperform. With Wipro', Wipro Annual Report, pg. 12-13, accessed 4 October 2019, https://www.wipro.com/content/dam/nexus/en/investor/annual-reports/2018-2019/annual-report-for-fy-2018-19.pdf

re-inventing ourselves and creating newer opportunities. This has been possible because of the deep commitment and hard work of Wiproites and the core values that have remained our guiding light.

Along the journey, we have focused on continuous evaluation of the capabilities we need to win. This year as a part of the strategic plan exercise, we identified four technologies that will lead us into the future—Digital, Cloud, Engineering Services and Cyber Security. Based on the approval from the Board, we have decided to step up our investments significantly in these four big bets. Furthermore, we also divested our data centre business which has improved our return on capital employed.

We are committed to enhancing value for our stakeholders.

Our EPS for the year ended March 31, 2019 grew by 18.6 per cent YoY, which was the best in the last 5 years. We improved our working capital substantially and our free cash flows was robust at 106 per cent of our net profits. We have a capital allocation philosophy of providing regular and stable payout to investors keeping two important considerations, one that of building long term stakeholder value and two that allows us to make required investments for future growth. Consistent with this philosophy, we declared a dividend of ₹1 per share, completed a bonus issue of one equity share for every three held in March 2019 and also announced a buyback of ₹105 billion through buyback to the shareholders in April 2019. The shareholders have approved the proposal to buyback equity shares of the company and the process is likely to be completed by August 2019.

As a large technology company which employs 170,000+ people, we have the responsibility to drive an inclusive growth. Technologies like digital and AI are disrupting the way services are rendered and the ability to learn becomes vital for our employees. At Wipro, we have made significant investments in re-skilling our employees in digital technologies. There are three levels of training that start from awareness programs, extensive learning programs through virtual labs and immersive programs that provide opportunities to build deep expertise. We are also using TopGear, our social learning and crowdsourcing platform as a workforce transformation tool as it has 2000+ learning assignments across 200+ skills. Today, we already have 55,000+ employees on TopGear. Localization is an important initiative we are driving to create a global, diverse and distributed talent base. In the last few years of running this program we have successfully localized all our major markets like the USA, the UK, Australia, Canada, Singapore, Africa and Middle East.

We are acutely aware that much of the economic progress in the world has come at the cost of climate change and therefore we have a responsibility towards creating a sustainable community. We have significantly scaled up renewable energy for our operations, contributing to 40 per cent of our total consumption. Recycled water now contributes to 42 per cent of our total water usage. Education has been the primary focus of our work for close to two decades now. Till date, we have partnered with 166 organizations working in school education. Wipro Earthian, a sustainability education program focused on water and bio-diversity, has reached out to 8,600 schools over the last nine years. The Wipro Science Education fellowship in the USA, which we started in 2013, works in seven sites across 35 school districts on improving STEM learning in schools serving disadvantaged communities. This year, we are collaborating with Kings College London and Sheffield Hallam University to provide rigorous continuous professional development to STEM teachers working in government designated 'opportunity areas' in the UK, which by definition have a high proportion of failing-schools.

Through Wipro cares, our employee giving program, we have worked on education for disadvantaged children and children with disabilities and worked with partners who provide quality primary health care services to underserved communities. My own thinking of wealth & philanthropy is that we must remain 'trustees' of our wealth for society, not its owners. As announced earlier, I have irrevocably renounced more of my personal assets and earmarked them to the endowment which supports the Azim Premji Foundation's philanthropic activities. The total value of the philanthropic endowment corpus contributed over time is $21 billion, which includes 67 per cent of economic ownership of Wipro Limited.

We remain committed to building a glorious future.

I am pleased to share that Rishad Premji, Chief Strategy Officer and Member of the Board, will take over as the Executive Chairman of Wipro Limited with effect from July 31, 2019. Rishad brings to this role new ways of thinking, experience, and competence that will lead Wipro to greater heights. He has been an integral part of the leadership team since 2007, and has a deep understanding of the company, business strategy, culture and heritage. He is also deeply committed to the values which form the bedrock of Wipro. I will continue to serve on the Board of Wipro Limited as Non-Executive Director and Founder Chairman while dedicating most of my time and energy to the philanthropic efforts of the Foundation.

Leading Wipro from 1966 till now has been the greatest privilege of my life, it has been an extraordinary journey. I want to thank the generations of Wiproites and their families for their contribution towards building our company to what it is today. I am grateful to our clients, partners, and other stakeholders who have reposed trust and confidence in us.

Wipro will continually transform to scale new heights as the world changes while remaining firmly committed to its values. I am confident that the future of Wipro will far outshine anything that we have done before.

Very sincerely,
Azim Premji

ACKNOWLEDGEMENTS

To my family, wife and daughters—who have supported and tolerated me patiently while I was immersed in writing this book...

To my forum—Akshay Batra, Amol Kapadia, Gaurav Jain, Kartick Maheshwari, Prashant Hingorani, Priya Kapur, Shripal Chowdhary, Vinati Saraf—thank you!